HOW ATTITUDE INFLUENCES WORK AND PRODUCTIVITY

Attitude + Work = Productivity

by Paul L. Reid

RoseDog Books

PITTSBURGH, PENNSYLVANIA 15238

RoseDog Books
585 Alpha Drive, Suite 103
Pittsburgh, PA 15238
Visit our website at www.rosedogbookstore.com

ISBN: 978-1-4809-8603-9
eISBN: 978-1-4809-8585-8

ACKNOWLEDGEMENT

I thank God for the inspiration, strength and health that He gave me to accomplish a special milestone in my life. I acknowledge the contribution of all those who helped me. You have played a role of influence in some way or the other to help me achieve my goal of writing my first book.

Special thanks to my family members for their patience and tolerance throughout the period.

Thanks to Franklyn who saw to the editing of the first draft of my manuscript. He complimented me on starting such a big project and suggested that I continue working on this book.

Thanks to all my friends, teachers, brethren and other cadre of company who encouraged me in realizing my goal.

DEDICATION

To my daughter Sheree, who is unique in persona, lovely in smiles and has a positive outlook on life. Sheree is an intelligent young lady, currently doing her degree at the Mona – University of the West Indies. She is very careful, especially in going after her goals and career path. I dedicated this book to her, as a source of motivation into the future.

To all the rest of the three children, that have their own special and unique personal attributes. Be persistent towards your goals, wearing the right attitude.

To all my friends, those that I met and will be meeting during the reading of this motivational and work-oriented book: may you enjoy the pages as you go through and discover some things you have never found out about yourself.

HOW ATTITUDE INFLUENCES WORK AND PRODUCTIVITY

Attitude + Work = Productivity

TABLE OF CONTENTS

INTRODUCTION

This is a fascinating book on attitude. It is designed for everyone to enjoy reading and exploring the ideas that this interesting title, How Attitude influences Work and Productivity, has to offer.

Attitude matters in everything we do. It affects our feelings, emotions, enthusiasm and mood display daily. This powerful word attitude activates the affective domain of our brain. This domain expresses the mood of a person's emotion, whether positively or negatively

So, you will recognize that this book is best suited for people of the working class, in industries, companies, and to some extent, the upper high school students in educational institutions. The concepts can be use in multifaceted ways in their application. They will improve their best practices, reshape work culture and transform young minds. They have the ability of shaping young people with a better work attitude in their field of work.

Furthermore, you can see for yourself how attitude has a great impact on workers, workplaces and locations around the world. Attitude has made a profound statement for decades in several companies and institutions at large, as regards to workers' output. These practical statements shown are in many ways like: how workers perform on the job; amount of work output; meeting targets; quota deadlines; and managing time overall. The speed at which productivity is carried out and how professionally we are approaching doing so is indicative of the result. The beautiful ideas presented in these chapters will bring you a wealth of knowledge and possible solutions to challenges faced.

I can assure you that these ideas will change the attitude of many workers in this twenty-first century. They will address peoples' attitudes or behaviors in different environs, especially, young adults in institutions, workplaces, and this competitive job market. New knowledge is more effectively used by people who have positive attitudes. But, it can only be powerful when utilized and transformed into real products. This school of knowledge is suited for the young people spanning across both genders.

This book has special features, which set the tone for people in the millennial era who will enter the workplace and those that are still in the working world. This concept personally developed for the working class emerges out of my scope of thinking. You will find the resource materials with fortitude of splendid ideas to break forth a paradigm shift in the landscape of the workplace. This concept is formulated like a Mathematical formula written as: $He+M+S+A = P$; it is called the Reid's concepts, which means High energy + Motivation + Speed/skills +Attitude = Productivity. This fabulous concept will be explained in details within the content of this exciting book, for the anxious go-getter and learners.

The content of this book seeks to elucidate the effectiveness of attitude: how good attitude can change workers and productivity in the workplace. Whether you read for information or fun, just read on; you'll find it interesting. Most employers will agree that attitude of workers plays a fundamental part of production; knowingly or unknowingly, it remains a fact. Everyone has an attitude and it is at the core of your mind, for example, emotions or feelings. You act out your emotions on someone or somewhere in a good or bad way. You expressed your attitude everywhere in your environment, where you may move or live.

Our attitude has an impact on work, relationships and family. You need to know how to use your positive attitude in your performance and productivity at every level. It is important that attitude be addressed and highlighted as the major ingredient that helps to drive performance in every workforce. So, what is positive attitude and negative attitude? Positive attitude is a good feeling expressed from the way you think or an opinion shared with someone and that is acted upon. How do they affect productivity? Positive attitude when displayed gives you a positive reaction: high performance, quality work and good production. This is the desired behavior required in the work environment. Negative attitude is the opposite; it shows a reluctant behaviour.

Therefore, negative attitude equals negative work output or turnover; tardiness reaching the company's target and deadline; employees who possess negative work attitudes and produce poor results; irrational behavior; complaints; and always blaming others for their failure. In chapter six, you will see highlights of five attitudes that drive workers to get peak performance at the workplace, for example; time management; the quality of work; speed; efficiency; and to a great extent accuracy, winning attitude and mental attitude. A man's thoughts become his actions. A human being reacts to a situation or a thing as a result of his thoughts transforming into words, then the ultimate actions.

CHAPTER 1

The power of positive attitude is an influential behavior a person passed on to someone. This influence has the ability to transform, negative thinking into a positive and captivating experience. This power of influence will change the attitude and actions of individuals into a more productive person in the environment in which he lives. Positive attitude is as a result of your power of thinking expressed in words. This is the reason a person's thoughts must be trained and be guided in a positive way. When this happens, man will experience a closer connection with his creator, people, and his environs. The creator is the one who inspired man with ideas flowing freely from his intellectual fountain.

Ideas will only be good if they are turned into real materials. They must be able to assist man to build a network of magnificent prospects of creating real jobs; empower young minds to do research and use creativity; and to develop dynamic products. This will, in turn, make us to be productive and better users of the scarce resources at our disposal.

HOW ATTITUDE INFLUENCES WORK AND PRODUCTIVITY

The power of positive attitude typifies an eagle's strength, which causes him to soar high in the sky. As you know, the power of an eagle lies in his far-reaching curved wings. This exemplary bird helps to teach us a simple lesson. One main lesson learnt is to use your strengths to overcome obstacles and gain supremacy over others. If you know your strengths, then you can soar high like the eagle. Utilizing your area of strength to benefit others, the sky is the limit, which means you have the opportunity to expand as far as you want to grow in your area of strength or business in life. You may not solve all of your problems in your life journey, but you may find solution for a part.

It is ironic to fathom the instinct, art and skills of the eagle: how the eagle utilizes his instinct in a witty way in comparison to our brain acuity. We have intelligence, knowledge and good strategies to face each day; to solve new problems and to encounter new experiences; to go through the rigour of life. But we do not use our strengths positively as the eagle. Let's think about the strategies of the eagle.

—◆—

Let's learn from the eagle; he operates from a high altitude so that he can vividly see those who are below him. He knows it is easier to conquer his prey when it's above him. The eagle takes less energy to fly down into a valley than to take off from in a valley to the mountain range. For a better description, we could say it is easier for an eagle traveling from a higher plain to lower than for the same eagle flying from the valley to a higher altitude. He will exert more energy going upwards on the mountain side.

Look! How smart the eagle's strategies are: 1. He uses height as a vantage point to operate from; 2. An eagle uses the strength of his wings to fly and manipulate its prey; 3. The eagle's eyes are magnetic and focused; it can see its prey from a distant. The eagle is a very strong and powerful bird, he uses his positive attributes to his advantage, which is its strength and power. An eagle eye is very powerful and magnetic. It identifies his prey from a far distance. It has positive attitude like confidence, strength and it always likes to conquer. Most of the time, an eagle flies high to position himself to gain superior advantage over the other birds or his enemy. It's no wonder why he separates himself to show that he is exceptional. He is a big bird in size; he has strong lengthy wings and he is bigger than the rest.

In today's world, there are several concepts, beliefs, and ideologies, which come across our minds. Some of them are very good and on the other hand, many are bad. You may just need to know how to train your mind to be positive, to achieve success in life. Learn to overcome our fears and use our strength to conquer our world. We need to possess a positive attitude and aptitude for us to reach our goals. There are five pillars of the power of positive attitude listed below; the key pillars are similarly a part of a person who possess good aptitude, which will position you to be on the cutting edge of time.

Five (5) key pillars of the power of positive attitude are as follows:

- Discipline
- Desires
- Wisdom
- Strength of character
- Persistence

IMPORTANCE OF POSITIVE ATTITUDE

Discipline is a systematic level of training, which changes your behavioural pattern. This training focuses the mind to think and behave in a particular direction. It is a specific moral standard of living, which is guided by our Christian principles. A disciplined person is one who is principled. He follows a set of clearly-written rules. He is able to apply training and coaching to govern his life. The Christian beliefs, educational philosophy and concepts help to shape him in how he should grow, irrespective of the cultural environment of today's world.

Discipline is the main pillar to the power of positive attitude. It has an impact on every field of study; for example, an engineer, mason, farmer, a teacher and an athlete. Every worker needs to be positive and disciplined. And to be disciplined you have to be positive. Every sporting activity, for example, basketball, netball, track and field are fabulous sports. They are played at the professional level and take positive attitude at all times to be successful.

Track and field and basketball are very lucrative sports. But, they require serious discipline to apply the skills and technique learnt in order to excel. Each game has rules to follow; if you do not follow the principles given by your coach, you will lose your space.

Breaking the rules of a game would be indiscipline, which cannot help you win in a team sports. In the history of the life of a legend, I have never read of anyone who was successful without being disciplined. Player-X, played golf; he was discipline in getting to be top as golfer in the world, Athlete-Y is one of the fastest 100 meters sprinters in track and field. It took him years of continuous training: that's discipline. Or else, he could not be the athlete holding the world record for the fastest times. In Cricket, W was one of the greatest cricketers of all time. He made triple century in a match for his team. It took him a lot of patience, hard work and dedication. But, most of all, the discipline of mind and physical body put together to achieve such great performance puts him in the hall of fame.

—◆—

Success comes through discipline, practice and repeatedly good behavior; this caused the behavior to become perfect. Good behaviors produce good attitude, and good attitude gives you the power of influence. Whenever a child is a high performer in his class work at school, most times, the teacher is motivated to use that child's work as a good example to show other members of the class. Sometimes that same child may be asked to be student leader of the class in the subject area. You see, this is influence, the power of positive behavior. You are rewarded for your good work. People who excells in their skill sets do not mind being disciplined. They know discipline is the secret weapon to success for reaching their goals in life.

Discipline is a quality which is trainable. You can learn how to be disciplined, just like how you can learn the winning ways in achieving a particular goal in life. It is harder doing the right thing or shaping the correct behavior in a person, than behaving negatively. For example, if you are earning from your job on a consistent basis, fortnightly, savings may be the last item on your priority list to do. You would prefer to buy food, clothing, and shoes instead of saving some of the money in the bank, for a rainy day. Well, this is just to show you how hard it is to discipline yourself in saving or being positive. Even if you were saving as small as 10% of your income, it would be a pain in the neck. Therefore, you can safely say, it takes confidence to emulate a positive attitude towards saving; it also takes good desire, persistent behavior and wisdom to save money successfully, in this tough economic climate.

THE GOOD DESIRES

Most people awake in the mornings with fresh desires, aspirations and wishes; while some wake up, but are dormant as the day they die. If desires could talk, they would speak to their faces, asking the question: what are you going to do with us? But, they are your intentions; they lie in the subconscious mind and someday wish they would blossom into lovely mature flowers, glowing into fruition, bearing fruits of all different kinds, probably looking on and smelling the petals of them all.

It is amazing to know that the numerous good ideas are sealed up in tombs of people with great intellect, who would never live to bring them into being or material wealth. They had wonderful plans, brilliant business proposals, beautiful architectural designs, millions of dollars of money invested, but these desires are now stifled and died a natural death. Oh! Good desires. What can we do? But hope, that at least two of them would just dream to us their ideas and go back to rest. How sad life turns for us? The environment that you live in helps to determine how well you strive.

Just imagine what some of these marvelous desires could be like: constructing the most beautiful scenery; a dream house in the middle of the ocean. Oh! This is like a living fantasy. I wished it was a reality. Good intents must be stimulated and encouraged so that they will spring up and grow into reality. Unless your intentions are clearly identified and are place in a fertile environment to be nourished, they will die. Positive words are peaceful, an uplifting energy which is sure fuel, that will be like sparks plug; it ignites the engine of the power of positive attitude.

Positive attitude is like an oasis in a desert. It has the water and nutritive values to grow and keep strong. It has the power to resist the negative energy around, soaring with authority, and influence to conquer. The beauty about positive attitudes is that they are infectious, lovely and irresistible. They have the attributes, worthwhile emulating by all human being of decades to come.

WISDOM

Wisdom is a positive word, which means to be clever, prudent and having-tact. The wisdom is also a descriptive expression to show how witty you are or can become. How prudently you use streams of knowledge and sound principles to harness wealth in your life is indicative of the result called wisdom. This powerful attitude, wisdom, is near in many individuals: your age may look like it; the brains do not think it; their speech doesn't express it; and neither do their actions display it. We may think that experience teaches wisdom; but, experience without knowledge could not equate to wisdom. Solomon in the bible was described as the wisest and richest man on earth. He had experience, power, wealth and all the riches amongst all the other men on earth in his time. He was a King of Isreal, humble, influential and good worshipper of God. If this man was not full of wisdom, he could not have accomplished so much wealth and greatness. I believe, it was his hard work, with sound principles, discipline and pure wisdom that took him to the top.

Wisdom is a discipline; having good desires and strength of character are three pillars of positive attitude. These pillars are enshrining the acts of wisdom. The ability of knowing how to apply wisdom and when to use it is an indication to prove that you are clever. Wisdom teaches you to listen carefully, when spoken to by someone. It respond gently, with wise words which have power and effect. Wisdom teaches you how to think and to act smartly.

Imagine! Who is regarded as a wise person? The people who are prudent and brave, those who take calculated risks and have strength of character. What do you think: the first man to travel to the moon or the first man to climb the highest mountain in the world, Mountain Everest? You may also say, "One of the fastest men in the world that came first in two consecutive times in an Olympic game." These men were not only first in their bid but they achieved greatness. They had the right attitude, thought wisely and their reaction time was positive and focused. The wisdom executed led them to the main stream to their success and history in the Guinness book of record.

—◆—

I wish to share five steps to wisdom with you, which are salient ideas to utilize in your daily life. They are as follows:

THE FIVE STEPS TO WISDOM:

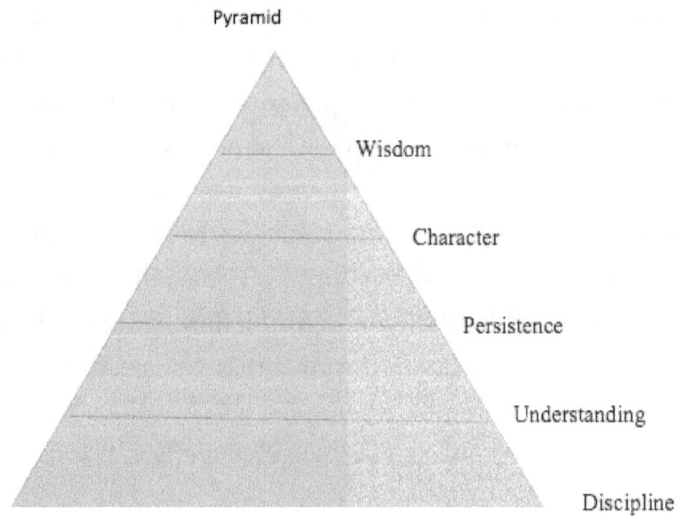

Pyramid

Wisdom

Character

Persistence

Understanding

Discipline

PERSISTENCE

Persistence is described as a behavior that allows a person to pursue something they need in life. It has the ability to survive the odds, whether the behaviour is set out to do good or not. It is firm in its actions and does not cease to happen. On a positive note, it was an exciting venture experienced in writing this book. It pulls out the attitude of persistency and discipline. To achieve my goal it takes time and effort to put pen to paper.

It takes patience to think of ideas and to put them together for readers so that they will be excited to read your book. Persistence is a quality needed in the workplace, and in every field of study, if you are to be successful. Each person must have an intrinsic motivation and courage to go all the way, in whatever you do. Persistence is a winning attitude you must adopt, even if you do not feel like you can make it. Try to endure and finish whatever you plan to do because the experience of winning is always sweet.

Being persistent is like a diamond in the rough, which takes time and patience to be cemented into a successful finish product. These five pillars of positive attitude complement each other; to be persistent you have to be disciplined, have good desires, be wise and possess the strength of character.

"Pursue your dream vigorously, make it your focus, and
do not lose sight of it. Write it down, activate it, when
the right time comes, builds it into reality."

—P. Reid

Whenever, you know you have a goal in view, you must pursue it with vigor and fixity of purpose. It is only when you exert the urgency of effort that others will see the need to help you along the journey. Reaching your goal is the ultimate. Sometimes, there are many mountains to climb, valleys to cross and lakes to pass through, but whether you swim or climb the mindset is the same: to accomplish your goal and that is persistent. The first and greatest woman swimmer from the Caribbean to get an Olympic gold medal took persistency and the P.U.S.H., which means Persist, Until, Something, Happens; that's what you need to do to be the next great record holder in your field.

STRENGTH OF CHARACTER

A person with strength of character has the ability to keep his integrity, possessing good qualities like honesty, courage, high moral and ethical values. These reputable qualities will help you to survive the difficult times. An individual with high morale is paramount for a personal repertoire in one field of work. When the morale of a person is high, he will be motivated and uplifted with energy, from a downcast spirit to power of strength. Winners do not quit, they possess inner strength, and willpower to do exceedingly above their potentials. They can bounce back from any fall or unfavorable possession to a higher plain.

A person, who exhibits strength of character has influence and good reputation in society. They possess a positive image that is intriguing worth emulating. Many saw individuals like these as the impeccable angel, who never changes his state. They have a good name, class and dignity. These exemplify the Queen, the Governor General, an Ambassador and others who exhibit good attitude. You can depend upon them to be your mentors and true examples.

UNDERSTANDING

The word understanding is one major step to the pyramid of wisdom. Understanding means to perceive, to grasp the meaning or idea of, to comprehend, or to have thorough or technical acquaintance with (Webster's dictionary). Readers are attracted to how words are placed in your story writing, articles and books, especially when they can understand its storyline, sequence of events, and its content in general.

But, most of all, readers love your story when it is written with clarity. Ideas written down must be thoughtfully placed, in the appropriate perspective. They must make sense, be understood and have their intended outcome, rather than placing idea aimlessly on paper, without organizing them in proper sequence that flows and make sense.

CHAPTER 2

"Mankind is a wonderful gift to creation; take care of him. Mothers are creator of creatures; don't harm them, for fear you destroy a possibility of blessing. They produce both good and the bad, to help balance life's equation."

—P.Reid

It is very important for each person to have an attitude of purpose, to know your purpose and fulfill your dream in life. We were created for a purpose, and design to function in a particular discipline or career in life. By extension, we use our career goals to share with others and to help our fellow men to achieve their goals and purpose too. If we simply try to find out: why we are here? Then, we would easily discover what our purpose is, and try to work in our purpose. For example, if you were created to be a doctor, then your purpose is to take care of patients, as a physician.

This field of study would definitely be the sciences, where you would have to know about the anatomy, biochemistry, physiology of the human being. You are destined to be a medical doctor after going through seven years of theory and practical training which would help you to pursue your purpose. This type of preparation of the mind is essential for executing your purpose. In this case, your mind has to be proactive, organized and sharpe.

Medical practitioners have three main principles to carry out in their field called the- Triple "S." Each S has a meaning. The first S means serving; the second S means solving and third S means saving lives. A doctor has the responsibilities of serving patients, solving problems and saving.

—◆—

Doctors are servants of the people; their customers are called patients. How well they fulfilled their purpose is dependent on the attitude they portray in getting the job done or to get the patient recovered from his condition. Are you with that proactive professional attitude? One who is compassionate, caring and sympathetic, working not only with the head and hands but with a heart of love and tenderness? Let us remember that, working with a sense of purpose and direction is a sign of positive attitude for achieving greatness. In order to fulfill your purpose, it comes with the right attitude in accomplishing your goal in life.

The human attitude is an expression of feelings, opinions, behaviors and ways of thinking. We express our feelings in different ways, like in our posture, how we walk, and gesture, in both print and electronic media spaces. Sometimes, they are displayed in our spoken words, written words or in action to get a desired result. Whatever way we choose to use them, the five senses help to transmit the message we send to our viewers, even in our body language or the silent voice. These attitudes we model, whether positive or negative, are an expressed image of a reflection of you the individual in the mirror of life.

These attitudes act as conduit of the five senses of man: feeling, hearing, seeing, listening and tasting. Whenever, a stimulus activates one of these senses, an attitude follows. We tend to show an attitude that is either negative or positive. Simply put, attitudes are originated from human beings' cognition, to be specific, the affective domain which relates to the emotion of a human being and how he reacts to people or things within his environment. For example, looking at the climate, it is sunny, you are able to move swiftly which reflects a mood of happiness on the face, but a cloudy condition cause a cold climate. You will have to wear thick clothing, feeling chilly and cold –seeing facial expression.

—◆—

One's mood of action to any circumstance is described as your attitude. Sometimes, when executing your job, the mood we wear hampers the quality and the rate at which work is done. A working environment which is calm, with a pleasant atmosphere, tends to foster productivity more than a boisterous and distracting environ. Many people do not concentrate or strive in noisy conditions; while some do not care less, they perform the same. There is a school of thought that states that: "your attitude helps to determine your altitude." This simply means, no matter how high you may excel in life; it is dependent on the individual work attitude. The amount of positive energy you put into your work will determine the fulfillment of your purpose.

WHY IS ATTITUDE OF PURPOSE IMPORTANT IN THE WORKPLACE?

Let's look at a scenario of my friend Ann, mother of Diana who started her education at one of the most prestigious preparatory schools in near proximity of about (5) five kilometers from home. Diana, in the first term of her school's work, performed well in all subject areas. But during, the second term of school, Ann noticed that her daughter Diana was not doing her homework promptly anymore; she was more engaged in playing games on her tablet or phone.

She tried hard to encouraged her to get back on track with her schoolwork, but this proved futile. Ann took away Diana's computer from her and threatened to give her less lunch money if she did not improve in her lesson. One afternoon, Diana came home, settled down to eat dinner and rest. She went to the drawing room to do some work. Later, Ann, went beside her at the table, while she was doing something, and asked her; "Diana, have you completed your homework?" Diana, looked at her Mom, rolled her eyes and looked at her through the corner of her eye, as if, she was saying, "Who are you talking to?" Ann, said, "Girl! Are you passing your place? Who are you giving attitude!"

Diana remained silent, while her mom was fuming in disgust at her behavior. As she calmed herself she said, "You know what? I will have to see your teachers at school to hear what is happening." The example, used is not only the essence of the reflection of attitude, but also an expression of behaviour, be it positive or negative or otherwise.

HOW ATTITUDE
OF PURPOSE INFLUENCES WORK?

As children, we grew up in a peaceful and fruitful little village. It was populated with people of a mixed abilities and ambitions. Some individuals' ways of life were varied from: farming, seamstress, mason, teachers and carpentry. Most of the citizenry career paths were farming; some did it as a hobby, backyard gardening and subsistent farming. These basic methods provided food for proper feeding of every family. Some people did mixed farming, which is the growing of different types of crops. This method includes rearing of small stocks like: rabbits, goats and chicken which help sustained the family unit with protein.

Subsistent farming is the process of growing catch crops and food crops in surplus; by extension the surplus is sold to people to survive the challenges of the high cost of living in the country. A matter of fact, these enterprises were industries created by community members, where people could feed themselves and earn a living at the same time.

During our formative years, every child was taught and grew up learning some skills through informal and formal apprentice programs. They learned life skills and how to perform their duties efficiently to meet the demands of the job market. In cases like these, positive attitude counts in order to fulfill your desired task in the workplace. In the formative years of every young life, it is critical that proper principles are learned and practiced by young folks. A common colloquial saying stated that: "It is better to bend the tree from it is young," which is true to most classes and category of living things. Whenever, young people are trained in basic principles very early, they will be better able to adhere to concrete information in later days. Similar to most communities then and even now, the boys in rural areas learned to care and manage the rearing of goats and sheep. In some cases a combination: the growing of cash crops like corn, peas, calloo, and cabbage etc. These were our business initiatives, in which we learned to take responsibility and be accountable for what we produced. Those who were fortunate as boys learned how to do plumbing, carpentry and construction work, while the girls learned to do seamstress and housecraft, etc. The brilliant brains went to training colleges, school of higher education and university.

—◆—

Interestingly, children had to learn some core values, like being respectful to elders, and attitudes of obedience to parents and leaders. We learned to be honest; honesty is the best policy. We also learned prayer and devotion to God and to be kind and loving to our neighbors. We were brought up in a strict way to use the social graces when it was necessary. For example: to say thank you when a person gives you something; excuse me, –when passing through a crowd or leaving a person's presence or a meeting; sorry, whenever you hurt someone or your belly may suffer bloating and flatulence passes spontaneously in the presence of friends or other company.

Mom taught us life skills: early to bed, early to rise, make you healthy and wise. It was an exciting moment waking up in the morning at 5 am to have family devotion with Dad, even if we did not want to. It was a must, you were not asked to do it, but it was compulsory. Though, it seems regimental, we enjoyed each moment. It did instill in us some the attitude of reverence and discipline. Devotion was like a push start; it helped us to start the day right. After morning prayers, we were off to the field to take care for the goats and other small stock on our animal farm.

On our way, there were buzzes of joyful noise along the journey, which made the distance become shorter. The siblings were so excited to go out at dawn. It was a team of us. I meant a cricket team. When we entered the farm, you could see us competing among each other, to milk the lactating goats. We took turns to learn the art of stripping the nipples of milk. It was a pleasure to drink some of the raw milk from the goat nipples. Keep it quiet, Mom must not know about this. We took the rest of milk home; mom used it to make breakfast and porridge for the younger siblings in the days. After milking, we moved the goats to green grass or pasture to be fed during the day.

—◆—

We took duties sometimes as fun. It was joy taking time to gaze on the beautiful pink or blue colored eyes rabbits while feeding them. My hand was busy lifting the rabbits, or rubbing their soft, smooth hair. This was like swallowing a tube of jello down my throat. While feeding these chickens at times, ee estimated their weights by lifting them up and speaking to them like children at school. Ironically, they would respond by keeping quiet, and then sporadically make sounds. Having said that, we were conscious of the time spent on the farm feeding animals. We would then prepare for school. Guess what? The routine would continue on our return from school.

We developed the attitude of love for doing duties timely, with positive work attitude, discipline of mind and a desire to achieve our goals in life without losing focus. There was no time or space for laziness. The girls had no escape route; they were streamlined to do duties. Work was cut out for them too: household chores, combing hair and dusting furniture, even if there was no dust seen. The order of the day was: washing dishes and doing other small duties, before bathing, eating breakfast and to set off for school.

The discipline to work was entrenched into our system: that hard work leads to success. Homework given from school by our teachers had to be done. This was no exception; all this work or a duty was routine for every day. But as children growing up, playing hide and seek, baseball, cricket or even dandy shandy had to be built in the scheme of the duties or else no work would be done. It is said "hard work and no play makes Jack a dull boy" and it was really so. Mom and Dad had better know how to deal with us. So, work was not a problem for us, while play or leisure times were a complement.

◆

Young people were more obedient to parents and the elderly then. They had the willingness to do duties and following clear instruction from older folks was a norm. Rebellious attitude was uncommon unless it was set up by someone or a group. Young adults were respectful, with proper decorum, and were more supportive and co-operative to authority and leadership.

HOW ATTITUDE OF PURPOSE INFLUENCES YOUTH

Young people like when they are engaged in meaningful projects or activities. They like to do things that will keep their fertile brains active and entreat the mind in critical thinking. Young people like science, to touch things, to feel and explore .They enjoy experimenting on living things in their own spaces. Finding out things for themselves and arriving at their own hypothesis and diagnosis is fun. Learning to take care of animals is one such activity that gives them a sense of purpose each day, and excitement.

We had a pet goat for our family; her name was Betty. A cross-breed between the Nubian and Mountain goat, she was the biggest goat among the herd of goats on our farm. My siblings loved to care for her. She was seen as a beauty amongst the rest of goats. She had a light brown band across her back and side and underneath her belly. Betty had a splash of white in her face and brown and white on the back feet. All the family members were happy for her; everyone enjoyed playing with her long white beard. They rode on her sunken back boastfully, for short moments on the farm. Lots of laughter filled the atmosphere, as she squatted obstinately, when she got tired to prolong the journey.

—◦◦◆◦◦—

Every morning and afternoon, we looked forward to seeing Betty and the rest of the herd of goats. Betty was exceptional; she was playful and affectionate, like rubbing her head on you when you drew near her. She would use her horns to butt at you in a jovial manner, in which everyone tries to run away from her. She ate feed out of our hands, for example, banana, breadfruit skins, grass and other fodder to nourish her body. We had pleasure feeding her, resting the palm of our hand on her two sprang horns, before putting her out on the green lush pasture. Betty liked to be fed with nutritious feed or else she refused to eat. As a matter of fact, her master knew what she liked and tried to provide the best feed for her.

We watched her grow in health to be one of the finest-looking small stocks comparable to none. She was seen as the best quality goat in the community amongst the rest. Betty was tame, easy to manage and to be fed. Betty had a big breast with two genuine conical shaped nipples, looking, soft and pendulous. She produced plenty of milk per week to supply the family needs and, at times, friends. She was rated as yielding the highest amount of milk per day, which was about one quart milk.

Betty showed off her worth as a miniature milking industry all by herself. She mothered two pretty kids that she gave the rest of milk and took care of them dearly all the time.

Betty's master trained her how to respond to her name when she was called, taught her the technique of hand feeding and involved her in playful activities. He also taught her how to socialize with people and be friendly. She was trained how to be conditioned and cope with milking operation, when she was being milked.

—◆—

Lessons to learn: your attitude of purpose has an influence on your learning and how you learn. There are different types of learners: Kinesthetic Learners learn by doing things; Visual learners learn by what you see; and Contact Learners learn by what you come in contact with. What you produce is dependent on what you learn. The productivity of a company is dependent on how much your employees learn and how fast you teach them. It also is dependent on how well they apply what you have learnt, which will enable them to produce profitable outcomes.

Young people can develop a sense of purpose and self-reliance. Working as a team can allow them to achieve their goals quicker. You must work and enjoy what you do. When you enjoy working at something you like, the task will be accomplish faster and better.

CHAPTER 3

"Work is therapeutic to life's problems. It is only meaningful when you plan and organize it. You focus on it, properly execute and experience it."

—P. Reid

The process of preparation is expressed in this amazing quote: "You can't push anyone up the ladder unless he is ready to climb himself," by Andrew Carnegie. Certainly not! This quotation speaks distinctively to preparation; let's reason, the ladder is simply the transport to assist you to where you plan to go. But, you need to know what you are going to do or gain at the end. You must know when you plan to climb the ladder and why? Preparing to go to work takes careful planning, for you to be purpose-driven and effective on the job. It starts with your attitude, you walk and talk with an attitude, and you work with an attitude too. We must also understand that there are various levels of preparation are done for going to work.

The first level is the beginning, the second level is the continuing, and the last level is the finishing. At each level, it takes different type of preparations. As a person, you need mental focus, physical fitness, endurance /stamina and motivation to go all the way to the finishing point to your job assignment. These three levels of preparation will take some form of mental readiness, where you will have to make decisions. The main thing to do first in this case is to create a plan of activity. It is your blueprint that will get you prepared for the day's work. This blueprint will guide you to know what to do, who to do what, when, where and how to execute your plan of activity throughout the time allotted to you for your task. The work you do each day begins with the strength of your mind, and it will be determined by how well you cope. Your physical health plays an integral role in work readiness. The combination of mind and body fitness will help employees to perform their plan of activity effectively. Bear in mind that efficient work accompanies good work attitude. Work is a way of life; it will keep you healthy and make you wealthy. It come with an attitude, you can either love it or hate to work.

WHAT DOES PREPARATION FOR WORK MEAN?

Preparation speaks to the readiness for work. It relates to being prepared to be engaged into an activity; you are ready to work on a task. The level of preparation is dependent on what you have set out to do. In preparing for anything in life, it takes a process. Proper preparation requires careful decision making, a planning stage, an organizing stage and an implementing stage. A fifth stage is the follow through. A positive mind to work is a very important attitude for an employee to have at all times.

Preparation for a day's work takes a mood of readiness, focusing on essentials things. Firstly –The worker must have the mind to work and the willpower to develop a desire and mental focus to go to accomplish the task ahead. It also takes the mental attitude and intellectual power to concentrate and to make critical decision. You have to plan activities necessary for work plus the day's journey. All of these ideas start with the power of your mind to think about and enact them.

The process of preparation will enter into four stages as mentioned above: planning, decision making, organizing and implementation.

Planning involves policy guidelines, which include decision making in all areas of our work. Every level of preparation you need to plan effectively, to be successful. But if you fail to plan, you plan to fail. No one wants to fail; everyone likes to succeed in whatever they are doing. Therefore, work your plan and put in all the things to be a winner.

Decision making is making choices; this is a regular part of our everyday lives. We make decisions in all aspects of our daily living at work and play. The decisions you make either make you or break you. It makes some people happy and some are made sad. Some decisions come by way of questions. There are many questions we ask ourselves, when we are preparing for work? What tools to take to work? Which taxi car to drive in? What should I take for lunch? And how will I make it to the next day and more...

- Secondly, Tools: Work men need to take the right type of tools and materials required to do the specific task at hand. Tools must be sharp, in good condition and functional: ready to be used. This will enhance preparedness and work efficiency in the workplace. It will allow you to gain superior advantage in the market place. Workers must practice to organize their tools, work space and themselves for a particular task. Whenever, you are professionally organized, put things in there proper perspective; it means that you are ready to compete with the best competitors on the international stage.

- Thirdly, Transportation involves an exciting venture of travel to mobilize workers. Some people who work commute on public transport or their private vehicle. The choice of transportation depends on how safe or comfortable they feel and the cost-effectiveness of travel. The choice of vehicle is dependent on the proximity and affordability. In any case, every worker has to reach his workplace on time, safe and in the best frame of mind. Whether you are commuting or driving your own vehicle, you must to reach to your workplace in peace for work. Most employees who work in factories are women; they like comfort and safety in travelling to work especially at nights. But, whether you are male or female both need the same treatment/privileges.

- Fourthly: physical application refers to the energy level or being healthy. The worker must be healthy with high energy that gives them the agility and fitness to work. Exercise is vital for blood circulation and muscle development and strength. Good mental and physical fitness will determine how effectively you will be able to execute the job.

- Fifthly: Skill-set- A good workman must have the right skill sets to fulfil the requirement for a particular job; he should be practicing his art frequently, so as to perform a high level of efficiency and proficiency at the workplace. Workers must constantly upgrade their skills and personal development. In a new world society as now, where the demand for computerized and technological skills proliferate in almost every workplace, the young people in the workplace must take advantage of this new landscape of technological skills available to them. They must equip themselves to multitask. The society we live in today not only promotes traditional jobs, but focuses on the higher-order jobs that need people who are of multi-intelligence can learn, such as multi-skills and logistical sciences. In doing so, it will put them in the limelight of being on the cutting edge of time. Generally speaking, they will be most often sought-after persons for many of these jobs, especially when they are properly trained in more than one skill.

The main point to success of an individual or the taskforce of a company is to prepare for work in any given day. One must cultivate the attitude of planning purposeful activity. This is an important element to start your day right. The sequence of activities or events is paramount for an effective day's work. You'll smile at what you did at the end of the day after you plan your activities to meet the needs for the day or in order of priority. It will be clear in his mind, how to allot time and energy to each hour of the day. Hence, this will make his day's work be productive as he planned it.

⸭

Each employee likes to see the accomplishment of all the activities he sets out to do within the day's work, without any difficulty. Every worker must try to develop a good work attitude. He must be organized in whatever he sets out to do. An employee must work according to his plan to be efficient each day. The worker efficiency will boost speed and productivity within the company. Practicing the skills required for each activity is key; it keeps you sharper for the job.

Managing your time right is always high on the agenda of every employer in a company you may work for. Good time management will charter a successful path in productivity and efficiency in any workforce. Being on time is a positive attitude to start your day right. Many employers prefer to see their workers entering the workplace on time, than coming in half of an hour late on the job. It shows respect for time and job. Employers like to see workers, trying to keep abreast with the schedule of activities for the company or planned task to be completed. This will give workers a full grasp or a better understanding of how to proceed in the daily task reaching company's goals. Otherwise, you would be towing the line of mediocrity and low productivity.

Workers who are organized and prioritize in their daily activities are more productive in work output than a sloppy worker who works randomly without purpose. Every smart worker makes a list of things to do, in an order of priority. This gives a clear path for the day's activity. Starting with the most important task to be done in a specific time allotted saves time and money. You are better off doing so. A person who manages himself and time well, he will manage his money better.

ATTITUDE OF ACCEPTANCE

CHAPTER 4

The attitude of acceptance is the ability of a person to be receptive to other people, their opinions or ideologies. It can be described as a warm welcome. The attitude portrayed by someone whether that of camaraderie or dissent of receiving others into your space in your company. This comes in different forms; a manager can accept you for a job in his company based on his standards. Acceptance may be due to your ethnicity, educational achievement, political or religious beliefs and socio-economic status.

The spirit of acceptance may be often highlighted as crucial to how someone feels about you. In many circumstances, your belief and culture play a pivotal role in some circles, whether, you will be readily accepted or not. For instance, an athlete who plays basketball very well, may be born in a first-world country but one parent is from a developing country. The manager might prefer not to take him on the team because both parents were not from a first-world country. He may have thought that he has more qualified natives, who are performing at higher expectation to choose from. There are many factors we can

HOW ATTITUDE INFLUENCES WORK AND PRODUCTIVITY

think of which may cause people to accept you. An individual will accept you because you are excelling in your career path. Some people may also receive you due to the fabulous name brand clothing you wear, your high intelligence and whether you are from an elite family or not. It is about your status code, profile and lifestyle. You must have the right fit or else you are a misfit and will get the red light.

Most people will give you the greenlight into their company when your profile fits the job criteria. But, human beings have the potential to adapt to almost every situation in life. They only need to orient their minds, to reach out to all men in their different groups and learn to embrace the attitude of love and equity, seeing each one of us are brother and sister. Then, we will be creating an atmosphere for everyone to be happy and feel cared for. All human beings are equal and should be seen as such on this earth. They must have access to all things and people in the universe, living in harmony as one people.

THE FACTORS CONTRIBUTING TO THE ATTITUDE OF ACCEPTANCE

This acceptance theory stated that: man may be received based on his beliefs, socio-economic status, family background, level of education, lifestyle, gender and attitude. People will accept you based on standards on what they know or practiced. It is possible that some people may even accept your ideas, but they do not receive you as a person because you are not an Oxford University graduate or from the right family.

This is equally true that a woman's job is in the home, although, she may have the highest level of educational capability. She fits the job title as the CEO / manager of a company, comparable to a man who may not be as qualified as her. But, he acquires the same job, because the management in that company sees the position as a male-dominate job. In this case, the preference is male; it is a man's job so the acceptance level for women would be zero tolerance, because, it would be a woman in a man's world. Today, society dictates a new paradigm shift from the old to a new concept, where gender differences go through the window.

We are living in the twenty-first century. The society has great young people who have new information and methods of management, to foster development in the new world order. We are more technologically equipped, computerized and have modern approaches. The present culture on technology has changed into the global village. The majority of CEOs of companies and institutions are either young male or female, managing with great competency and efficiency into productivity. There are new and different ways of doing things now; every day new techniques and research are unfolding before our eyes.

The acceptance level in our workplaces today varies; people use different meter stick to judge you. Some people may judge you by the address you are living, the lifestyle and, socio-economic background. If you are performing in a company, it does not matter where you are from. But, frankly speaking, quality performance, efficiency and productivity are the real deal.

HOW ATTITUDES OF ACCEPTANCE IMPACT THE WORKPLACE

It is quite observable to see the faces of employees and attitude portrayed in the workplace: the body languages, reactions to their co-workers and the supervisor. The attitude tells how they are feeling and what they are experiencing on the job. In some workplaces, you feel like something resonates through the room, when they are happy at work. Workers look pleasant having good work relationships among each other while effective work is still going on.

On the other hand, if employees are disgruntled, the mood at work become melancholy. While you may not see much active work in progress, it's another side of your mood. A person's mood is a part of the core of a person's emotional intelligence, which may be called the Affective domain. Some people celebrate you, while others do you hurt and don't, even care less whether you are affected by what they say or do. But, anyway, that's a part of life.

We know as human beings that everyone acts or reacts towards each other in a different ways. It does not matter whether we are male or female, rich or poor, whichever side of spectrum; all humans exhibit sometime a positive or a negative attitude. In any case scenario, employers are more receptive to an employee who portrays positive attitude towards his work, than a negative attitude. They like to see skillful, industrious and impactful workers who produce efficient work for their customers.

Management of companies are always with an attitude of expectation of their employees; they look to them for high quality and standard performance in all areas. Likewise, every worker needs high energy, self-motivation, speed and accuracy to achieve great success. But most of all, a positive attitude is the driving force behind a worker's achievement, that's what counts. A high level of energy speaks to a healthy person who is ready to work, as you say the word go. One can be either intrinsically or extrinsically motivated to work at their best, which means you are inspired by self, people or things in the environment. It could be how facilitating the workplace is or the equipment provided at work. Similarly, employees, like managers, have attitudes of expectation in regards to incentives, promotion, salary packages and other benefits given.

Your attitude is everything you think when you develop an opinion or feeling about people and things in your world. Although, the opinion you form about a person does not define him. Neither can you define a person by how bad you think about him. How do you see yourself at work? If you are the energetic, positive and graceful person, then you may be the right person who will wow the boss with good work attitude.

HOW ATTITUDE OF ACCEPTANCE AFFECTS PRODUCTVITY?

The attitude of acceptance is a principle or guide whereby standards are set by the company's management, in order for the receiving and sending out of products from the company. Workers are the creator of products and the quality produced is dependent upon the maker of it: how well the producer sticks to the company standard. The skills displayed at times come either from a good attitude or negative attitude, which helps to determine the quality.

There are clear standard uses to make products. For example, designing a bag will take accurate shape, style and pattern. The use of information like size or correct measurement will be necessary to give a perfect finished product. The texture and type of materials are key elements to boost the quality and quantity production.

How skilled you are in producing quality bags within a specified time, for your company will be a reflection of your positive work attitude. Also! how to keep a deadline for fulfilling quota, sales of products and your business arrangement.

Use the information you read from the chapters of this book to fill in the most suitable answer/s to your question: Then, see if there are ideas you have gleaned which could help you to make a greater success in your life.

1. What is meant by attitude of acceptance?
2. How does attitude of acceptance affect your work?
3. List four qualities of attitude of acceptance.

THE MIND TO WORK HARD

CHAPTER 5

Mental attitude is the most power attitude; the human being has to direct the entire functioning of the body. Man's mind is at the seat of his intellect, his thought process. From the inception of man in creation, he was created a thinking being, he thinks and acts from his mind. He was designed to work and that was part of his primary function. So, we can safely say, it is an inborn desire for man to work. It is man's responsibility to earn a living. He was made to have dominion over the universe and take care of it. He was created to manage his environment and to see to the success and productivity of what he does. He had no other choice for survival; work is a way of life.

There are two main principles to work: mental attitude and physical attitude. The concept of the two is interdependent; mental controls the mind and physical controls the body but the body is dependent on the mental attitude and vice-versa. It is an attitude you can either like or do not like. For mankind to survive and live a healthy and prosperous life, he has to work hard for his bread on this planet called earth. Man has the willpower and the intrinsic motivation to do what he sets out to do. The will to work is always there; it just needs to be motivated.

The desire to work hard comes with an attitude. It is not work at a normal level. For example, if you are a self-employed seamstress who decides to work hard to complete a task, let's say, making a dress for a friend in two and half hours for a special occasion. Let's call this job "push work." You must imagine that it will take more energy, speed, accuracy and concentration to produce a dress of high quality finish. The mindset of the worker, along with good skills application is vital in such venture. This will take an extra effort, to do a successful job. Work is made easy when you are competent in your area, producing a quality result and you like your job. Spending quality time in comfort, having an inviting environment, propels you to perform at your best.

On the contrary, when you are employed by a company it is different; you work on demand or the instruction of company's deadline. Push work is not given to everybody, but special categories of workers whom the manager knows have that good work rate, attitude and manage well. Sometimes, these employees are the middle-manager, who displayed the attitude that expresses a business-like approach and a cut above the rest of workers.

—◆—

Most of the times, individuals who are privileged to these opportunities are already benefactors of company benefits, for example, housing allowance, car upkeep, transportation allowance, vacation leave and even entertainment package.

Every human being has a fun side or a social attitude as a part of their lifestyle. Where the workplace comradery and harmony exist, you will find productivity excels. I believe in working hard but equally also to work smart. In every company or factory, there should be a concerted effort made to have a least one hour for relaxation either fortnightly or monthly. This occasion could be at different times. Employees who like playing games, listening to music or motivational audio/ speeches could be gainfully occupied learning while enjoying themselves.

It has been proven in many workplaces, where some form of leisure time is given, more output of work is produced. The employee morale to work is on a high. They are motivated to go back to their job in a better frame of mind the next day.

Let us discuss. Five key factors that contribute to working hard:

- Mental attitude.
- The desire to work.
- Physical fitness
- Good health
- Motivation

WHY IS IT IMPORTANT TO WORK HARD?

"Enjoy what you do! Work is like a medicine; you need to take the right dose. It is a therapy; relax while doing it. For it is a solution to your physical and financial needs rather than a problem."

—P. Reid

Working hard is a concerted effort made or high energy exerted to accomplish a task on a project, when you have seen the completion of what you set out to do. You feel a sense of fulfillment and finality to your work. Hard work starts with a deep desire to be successful, so you have to develop the high energy level and courage to be gainfully occupied. Everyone works, not only to be active but to achieve a particular goal. This goal may be a financial, to make provisions for the family, for children's education, to make a nice house, and to do business. These are dreams and more that we seek to attain for ourselves and others.

One's desire is his wish, passion, or a longing to be fulfilled by something. You can either have a desire to work or to have fun, but the two cannot work at the same time. For example, Ruthven likes ice-cream; for a long time her mother did not buy an ice-cream for her as dessert. So, she started crying in pretense and caused her mouth to salivate profusely to the floor. This was a sure sign of expressing her desire to have the ice cream to satisfy her wants. You know mother's heart is soft, so in a jiffy, she got the ice cream. Ironically, this was a long time promise, for work already done.

A desire is an innate feel wanting to do something: it's an ego that puts you into a reactive motion to realize a task. Your inner feeling exhibits sentiments shared, how things are happening for you. They can be either sad or joyful experiences, which cause an attitude to pop out on your persona. Sometimes, you wish this never to appear like it did, but you just can't help it. It is like when you wake up in the mornings; sometimes you may not feel like your true self or call it vibes; intrinsic motivation may not be there. So, you have to lift yourself up, with some vigorous exercise to get going or for the drive to work.

WORKING HARD IMPACT PRODUCTIVITY

Physical fitness relates to a process by which the body undergoes exercise to get flexibility in every lymph, muscle, joint and body part. The active movement of all body parts without undue stress is regarded as fitness. Physical fitness is vital for good mental health, body composure or relaxation, proper blood circulation and heart function. Fitness also is important for enhancing enzymatic and metabolic process to take place in the body. You are better at your work when good physical health is achieved. You express your feelings, talking and moving around with more energy. The amount of work done will be dependent on how well work was executed. But it is the high energy and fitness of the worker which eventually impacts output or productivity in the business.

A physically fit employee is a more productive person at work, especially, if they are eating nutritious and balanced meals and drink to boost energy level. An employee who sets out to eating balance meals, with the right amount of calories, minerals, vegetables and nuts will yield a desired result. Most people like to feel good and look good about themselves. Your health

and your look lies in the type of food you eat, which is your medicine. Physical fitness is compatible with your health. Hence, an excellent workout and a lovely drink will enhance the energy level you need for the day. Some folk are hyper, especially, if they know their fitness is up! They walk with an attitude about themselves. They move with agility. And, posed with an attitude of a peacock, act as if they will conquer the world.

One afternoon, a friend and I were having a causal drink; soon or later we diverted to talking about physical fitness and flexibility. Would you imagine, after having such invigorating discussion, that friend tried to challenge how flexible I was? At first, I thought he was joking but, alas! I saw him straighten up, took his hands over his head then, stretch to hold his toes for about five seconds, sitting on the floor.

I laughed with a loud voice! "Very good, your fit man!"

He laughed and said to me, "It's your time now."

I was a little apprehensive but, in order, not to let him think I could not do it, I said, "Okay! Watch me now." I laid on the ground, stretched out my hands above my head, then took my hands to hold my toes for even longer than his time.

He was in astonishment to see how his boastful attitude actually lulled in shock! He said, "Well you beat me to it. Congratulations! I learned my lesson; never again will I underestimate anyone." Thanks my friends, you see, don't try to test a book by just looking at its cover. I proudly explained how I did aerobics in the morning and evening along with physical activities that work for me; that is why I am so flexible.

On the contrary, some people thought going to the gym is the only solution to an individual's fitness, whereas, your daily chores with rigorous activities can develop into meaningful exercise, keeping you fit with alacrity and poise.

A PERFORMANCE DRIVEN WORKPLACE

CHAPTER 6

A performance-driven workplace is a culture where employees are given task work and pay by performance base. This involves on-the-job training and performance management, where you are graded according to work quality, speed and accuracy at which work is completed. Reports on data collection and evaluation of employee work are done. A reward system for performance of employees is also put in place. There are several factors that drive performance at most workplaces. There is a stringent management system to supervise small groups of people. For example, like middle managers who oversee medium sized groups of workers say ten to twelve people and micromanagers who may just have six workers to supervise. These systems put in place help to safeguard better supervision of line staff and lower category workers, accountability, workers quality, production and equipment etc.

The worker's morale is an important factor to performance; whenever an individual worker like his job and is happy, he tends to work harder. If the vibes are low, the turnover of work is equally low. All workers enjoy seeing very good working environments good ergonomics, where equipment, technologies and tools are placed correctly, accessible to workers and in good working condition.

Workplaces where management cares for their employees' welfare and performances are generally high. If the pay is good and a fair incentive system is in place, productivity will boom. Most employees like recognition, gifts, and awards because they will allow them to feel better motivated and satisfied that someone appreciates their worth. Anything that will change the employees' standard of living or self esteem means much to them. The two major catalysts to the engine of performance are rewards and incentives; especially, if it is financial incentive. This drives workers crazy to get the task completed in record time. Overtime work also creates a shift in the mental attitude of employees to achieve more money.

Every employee in a company wishes to get a good pay package at the end of the work week or month. During these times, the paid employee's attitude changes; when the salary is improved, his morale is high. The employee feels accomplished when he can pay his bills, feed his family, to give the children a good education and build his dream house. Working to acquire a large sum of money or small amount of money: both extremes come with an attitude in every employee behavior.

The attitude of empathy must be shown to those that get a small salary. Many times they are left to face the music of bills overload and deficits; this cannot balance out at the mini-mart. There are so many variables that can be a factor in the equilibrium: where performance, work output and ultimate remunerations for employees are a concern. Let's address these matters.

THE FACTORS THAT DRIVE PERFORMANCE

Motivation is a driving force to work performance, output and productivity in any company. Well-motivated employees are more creative and productive within a company when given a task to do than a demotivated employee. Motivation is the main factor to performance, improvement of quality, and ultimately productivity in our world of work. Job performance is based on your ability, skills and knowledge of your work to produce the desired result.

Some workers are intrinsically motivated to do work, which is natural from within; they are born with that good work attitude in whatever they do. But some people have to be push started by external motivation before they can produce a significant amount of work.

External motivators may give rise to threat, effective discipline or punishment, incentives, positive reinforcement, promotion and setting work-related goals. Some people are externally motivated by other outside factors, for example, workplace environment, lunch room, sanitary convenience and aesthetic value of the surroundings. Having good working conditions, pleasant workers' inter-relationships and positive team-work building, than one of poor acceptance and complaint.

Every employee likes a good, clean environment to work. As the colloquial saying is: cleanliness is next to Godliness. Employees like to know that management treats them as human beings while they perform efficiently to take care of the company's productivity. When an employer allows workers to feel like they are part-owners of the business, it lets them feel upbeat or excited and ready to perform at their best.

Every employer is always looking to see each employee approach his or her work and workplace with a sense of purpose, energy and focus on the job. They must be with strong mental concentration, positivity, and enthusiasm to do an effective day's or week's work.

HOW CAN ATTITUDE AFFECT PERFORMANCE AND PRODUCTIVITY?

Some very important fundamental factors workers need to know when entering the workplace are as follows:

FIVE FUNDAMENTAL ATTITUDES
THAT INFLUENCE PERFORMANCE.

Time Management is a key element of efficient functioning on the job coupled with work output. If an employee puts in more time on the job, it will create a better work rate, working relationship with the employer, and better result. Proper time management on the job makes you look professional, highly respected and dependable. You will be admired as a trendsetter and a good example to be emulated. Time management is a skill that is learned; managing work and yourself is just as important to performances on the job. Be professional by setting up a work to-do list and organizing it in order of priority. Eliminate the less important ones, then place the others in order 1- 3. Start with the most important one. Put timing into each piece of work.

Work Quality is a high standard of excellent performance delivered by an employee. The quality of work produced has a positive impact on productivity of any company. If you were to run a survey of all CEOs or managers, it would be their quest to see excellent quality and large quantity of produce on a consistent basis in their company. Whenever a worker produces quality products, it's the employer's delight. Producing quality work will ensure worker job security, he will get better pay and recognition, hence, achieving the goal of the company and securing preferential markets.

Positive image is the good picture each employee paints on the job. The worker who models positive image plays a pivotal role in representing the good image and ideals of their company. Employees must be prepared to carry out the company's work ethics, and maintain quality and the standard required. They must adhere to the company's dress code, culture, good communication and interpersonal skills, and decorum among all categories of workers. This show off what the company stands for.

A company's image is not only defined by what it produces and the company's trademark but by its reputation, track records, plus its quality of goods and services offered. The societies judges and compare you among other companies and you will be given thumbs up if you stand out as one of the best.

Speed refers to how fast you as a worker can produce a quality product in the shortest possible time. Completing a task with a high level of accuracy in a quick time exemplifies you as an efficient employee who knows what you are doing. For example, a bakery has one baker: will he be able to produce ten baked breads in less than one hour? But, if you have two bakers you may be able to produce more bread in lesser time, because you will have more work done by more hands at a faster rate and work output.

Efficiency is the ability of the worker to utilize the minimum resources available to him to produce quality products in the fastest possible time. Employee efficiency on the job depends on the skill sets executed in their field of work. It also depends on how effectively you can use your skills, with the limited resources and time to create quality products, with accurate menstrument and excellent productivity.

These five factors mentioned above combined together, when applied to the workplace conditions will set the employee in a good stead to approach the workplace. These factors if implemented will yield maximum result to your business. The highest performance is what each company needs from every category of worker to drive productivity. It is not just what you say that counts but what you do. Your work will speak well of you and yield the desired result as a team.

WHY POSITIVE ATTITUDE IS IMPORTANT IN PERFORMANCE

The success of every factory relies on the positive work attitude of the individual employee. A performance-driven workforce demands positive attitude for productivity to be realized in a company. The taskforce in a company has to be guided by the logistics of the principle of supply and demand for its products. To achieve company requirement it takes discipline and persistency in producing quality products, meeting deadlines and proficiency at the workplace. Employees' positive attitudes are contagious and have great influence on other workers to drive the production for good performance in the workplace.

Most companies' management always seeks to keep high-performing workers on the job because they are the live wire and go getters with the positive work attitude to make the company dreams comes alive. Having high caliber employees means producing products that can compete with international standards.

CHAPTER 7

"'Thank you' is a magical statement, which leaves a positive impact on the mind of the giver. It expresses a hearty feeling of affection for a kind deed done, which is better than one million dollars given as a prize, or a show of riches at a grand gala."

—P. Reid

The good master of the universe has placed a part of Himself in every man. This is His spirit of love which is expressed in our emotions. He has commanded us as human beings to give thanks for everything He gave us. We must show gratitude for life and the creation, which includes animals, plants, sunlight, water, oxygen and all the things that make up this beautiful environment. It is an acceptable norm to give thanks for the good things and bad things likewise because, He created them all for us to experience and learn from them.

People express their gratitude in different ways, for example, for waking you up this morning, breathing a breath of fresh air. If, in five years of your working life, you were able to buy a new BMW car, then, you would have achieved something. This made you happy that you can celebrate with family and friends. Not many people owned or have the ability to afford a car of such BIG brand name so, giving thanks with an attitude is justifiable. Be grateful for small mercies.

We tend to say thanks for good things which happen to us but forsake the unfortunate ones. I cannot see in my wildest dream why you should want to give thanks for a condition where your spouse had breast cancer, and waiting to do surgery to amputate her left breast . . . would you give thanks? This is ironical! You should be grateful to watch your spouse walking around with one breast? Or whether, to praise the surgeon for a splendid job done, to cut the breast off- no!

—◆—

In truth and in fact, it is a mind game: how we think about people, things and situations. Our perceptions of things allow us to take a stand, which can either be negative or positive attitude.

In the context of the spouse infested with breast cancer, humanly to see such condition and give thanks would be bizarre of me. Except, that her life was saved after the doctor performed a successful surgery. Then, her life being spared to live again as a normal person with all mental faculty intact, she has the capability to be a productive citizen once again. It would be rather prudent and also fair to show gratitude to the creator in the face of adversity for progressive healing and deliverance. Some people may not understand how thanks should be expressed in the face of adversity. But, for every ounce of healing, it deserves a pound of praise and in every pound of praise, there is a crown of glory. There is a science to life and a hope in a heart with an attitude of gratitude.

Let's put on our thinking cap, because sometimes out of every bad situation, there can be good things that jump out at you, that resonates for life. These good things most times are the secret, to mine gold. These secret may be your desires, your persistence and determination to go after your dreams in view. They allow you to feel closer to reality, to express much gratitude! And you will still be correct if you use the golden rule: in everything give thanks. As you progress step-by-step into fulfilling your dream. Every positive well thinking person, in most cases, will verbally express an attitude of gratitude for his heartfelt life. This can be a breath of fresh air we breathe, for the job, family, friends and the clean environment in which we live in and operate. There are numerous things not mentioned, which equally deserve our gratitude. But let's pause here, and reflect to see if, we left the most important thing for the last.

——◆——

It's a happy feeling and a sense of gratitude, one day seeing the bright sparkling sunshine bursting through the cold winter climate on Main Land Street. My heart is warmed to experience sitting in the sun on my cousin's front verandah in a temperate climatic condition, in a foreign country, the land of opportunity. My goodness! What a sudden transition: a few minutes ago I felt warmth but alas! It's now chilly and cold shimmering, all clod in my winter gears. Ah! What a change in temperature!

Well! I know, it will not always be sunshine, neither will it always be rain; but I know sometimes it will be warmth and could also be cold. Whatever, time it may be, give thanks! Because, He gave us both at times, the sunshine and the rain. Let us strike a balance; do you know that life consisted of both good and evil? Or positive and negative circumstances. Since both experiences are equally important, let us be objective and react to each challenge with an attitude of gratitude. Life is a dynamic experience with the two extremes of good and evil. Let's face it with a beautiful smile, and a stunning attitude of gratitude. They were placed in our midst to make us to be wise in choosing our destiny. There is never one without the other.

Most parents and grandparents in former years liked to pass on to the millennials etiquette. These golden principles are rich in many cultures, and they form part of the social fabric of society. Social graces are little ethical principles or what I would call magic words; they will help you to get by life's hurdles better. For example, kindly say: thanks or thank you whenever, something is given to you or when someone has done something for you. You do not have to be a bully or coarse person to command respect. In case, you need to say something while another person is talking or he is standing in you path, just simply say: "Excuse me. I am sorry." Please forgive me, is right in order. If, you have wronged someone, repeating any one of these magic words /phrases in the appropriate context will create a good atmosphere to ensure a positive attitude and good human relationships. Furthermore, your acceptance level will be better and highly appreciated.

FIVE BENEFITS OF THE ATTITUDE OF GRATITUDE
- It brings satisfaction of accomplishment.
- It stimulates a mood of happiness.
- It fulfills a purpose and replicates into other blessings.
- The magic word "thanks" transmits positive reaction.
- It sets a platform for opening doors to opportunities.

In the Jewish culture the magic word "thanks" or "thank you" was a common place for each person to say thanks after a good deed was done to them. The Christian teaching adapted the same principles as a profound and applicable attitude in our Western context as Judo-Christianity doctrine. The Good Master taught the story of the ten lepers who sought after Him because of His power of healing, virtues and prose in His ministry of healing.

They were overwhelmed seeing him in a particular village, moving through with alacrity towards the Master and cried, "Lord have mercy upon us," with bended knees worshiping him. The master instructed the lepers that they should show themselves to the priest. They did obey the command; as a result their leprosy were cleansed. Their skins were all recovered to the former glory of youthfulness or like a baby. But, only one leper returned to the Lord, with a loud voice of gratitude and appreciation to the Master for the miracle of healing. He fell on his face and worshipping, giving thanks, The Lord asked him the questions: "Were there not ten lepers cleansed? So where are the nine?"

—•◆•—

The good Master acknowledges the attitude of gratitude the leper portrayed. The remarks he gave in affirmation fulfilled the completeness of the lepers' healing when He said, "Go, your way your faith has made you whole." This miracle leads to an indifferent or negative attitude of indignation from other people in the village. Nevertheless, the job was already done and the desired result deserves high praises.

THE LESSONS LEARNED FROM THIS STORY OF THE LEPERS ARE:
- Whenever you are in need, it is important that you ask for help from the right person.
- The Master honors and rewards anyone who possesses a grateful attitude.
- It is wise to be obedient and show respect to authority.
- It is best to follow good instruction from a wise person.
- Be humble and patient in difficulties circumstances.
- Have faith and confidence in the creator in every situation

Showing someone that you are grateful or to say thanks is a deep sense of appreciation, and worth for work done by such person. It is this magic word "thanks" that can move the heart of an individual to do extraordinary acts of kindness. Thanks is a social grace; when you use it in context, it makes a gracious connection with you and people, thus opening doors of opportunities for repeated positive responses. This means you command the respect of the persons who display these deeds of kindness to you. When gratitude is exhibited, it brings satisfaction to you; it also forces you to think deeply, trying to find out what you have done well. Opening your scope of thoughts in your mind to see how much more favors you could grant to others of similar nature.

Attitude is in everyone and it reacts in your presence in any space. It affects the higher class of animals and lower. For example, a horse wags its tail with pride and composure alongside his master after winning the 10 kilometer horserace. Here the horse is simply expressing a winning attitude and appreciation to his master for allowing him to run and win the race.

While on the other hand, one of the greatest cricketers who made double century walked with his bat with great sense of accomplishment at Lord's cricket ground. The spectators cheered in the pavilion as they became a part of history. Sometimes attitude can be situational due to the place where it was shown. The way one acts at the Mary Mount High School may be different at a similar high school for example, at George Gibson Memorial High in terms of behave, learning outcome and the level of performance. This attitude of gratitude is of high value; It transcends sporting, educational barriers, and ethnicity, and is irrespective of your cultural flavor or background.

How fast or slow an individual functions is dependent on the facilities, time period and the situation. We must be thankful at all times in spite of whatever, state we find ourself in. The good book embraces the spirit of gratefulness in all things. But how many of us practice this golden rule to have an attitude of gratitude whenever we are going through rough times or our valley experience in our life? Do you approach the bad situations with a positive attitude? Greeting your problem with a spirit of gratitude coupled with a smile? That's the best approach for you to face life: to conquer your negative circumstances with a positive reaction.

Try at all times not to think of the problems, but use your energy to think about solutions to overcome the circumstances. Then, you will have half of your problem solved. Often times, we are joyful with great energy and pride, when most things are going right for us. So, why not use this strategy of finding solution first, instead of worrying? It will be worth saving your energy and just give thanks!

HOW ATTITUDE OF GRATITUDE IMPACTS WORK

Children are going to school and doing fine in their education. But at times mishap does occur; take for example, mom and dad at home, suddenly one of them fell sick. Then that attitude of gratitude may not be expressed, because it is a bad experience for the family. There is nothing to smile about or give thanks for. Neither parent is able to work to earn money and muster the strength to take care of the children. When things like these happen, it comes with an attitude of sympathy for the victim of sickness. Because of the inability to work, it poses a challenge to the individual and his family. This is a variable that you did not need to put in; although, it has the possibility to change.

It is like living in a temperate climate now; you may enjoy the sunshine for what it worth- because it might change in moments to snow!

But whatever time it changes to, let's be thankful, because each condition comes with benefits. The Master of the Universe has a way to reward people who are thankful. People feel fulfilled when you convey gratitude to them. In this context, the law of reciprocity is expressed in such a way that some other good deeds are meted out to you again. Thanks is a magical word that gets quick response, which always brings positive benefits to the recipient.

One day, I was perusing on the busy main street of a city when I met an old man begging money to buy food for his lunch. I told him I had no money, but he insisted, begging sorrowfully: "Please! Give me what you have."

I gave him a patty I had for myself.

He replied, "Thank you." But he stood still waiting. So I asked him what else he needed, he quickly said: "A drink." My heart melted instantly' the magic words, thank you, made it unavoidable. I had to give him the drink I partial utilized. I literally, saw his face light up, with smiles all over, as if he had one of the greatest gifts. I was astounded to see how he walked away, joyful with his meal. I was one of the happiest men too. This experience left me to believe that, in every stratum in society, there is someone who is less fortunate than us. So, giving thanks for where you are, it is not an option now. You just need that burning desire and the mind to work your way up and out of the situation by taking action without complaining about our status in life.

DISCOVER YOUR MEMORY POTENTIALS

Use the information you read from the chapters of this book to fill in the most suitable answers.

Questions:
1. What is an attitude of gratitude?
2. How does the attitude of gratitude impact work and workplace?
3. List four lesson learned from the story of the leper.

CHAPTER 8

"For your dreams, to become a reality, you need to visualize it, identity with it, and put purpose to it. Work on it and claims it; then it will become yours."

—P. Reid

Work is the application of force to an object, which moves in the same direction; you may also describe it as an activity that takes mental and physical effort to perform a purpose or a task. Rate is defined as a numerical proportion between two sets of things or variables. Let's say, for example, an athlete who is a hundred metre sprinter travels at 80 kilometers per hour, while another athlete will run as a sprinter at 70 kilometers per hour. These two comparisons are showing a difference of ten kilometers. The reality is one of the athlete covers the 100 kilometers distance, in 10 kilometers per hour faster than the other athlete. This clarifies the fact that the person who is faster showings a better work rate over the other.

Every work challenge may require a different level of effort and time. So, it is very important to have an idea of the type and volume of work you have to do and the approximate time, it will take to accomplish the job. Some types of work take more physical effort than mental, as well as others may take more mental effort to solve the problem. The direction, in which these two efforts go does not really matter. The essential thing is to be prepared so that you will make good use of the time. The modern workplaces and employers demand efficiency at work. This simply means each worker must be physically fit and mentally sharp, which is the hallmark to achieve high productivity in a quick turnover.

Employees need to orient themselves before entering the workplace and keep abreast of the main requirement for their specialized area of the job and learn them quick. This makes their transition into the workplace smoother with less hiccups. Therefore, having the prerequisite skills and a higher rate of productivity will be realized working in any company. Each worker will be more efficient and competent at everything they do. They should be excellent in all areas of their work life, thus improving themselves in personal development, multi-skill dynamics, highly motivated attitude, and willingness to work hard and smart in their field of work. Employees must take responsibility to make strategic moves to improve performance and work rate attitude in the workplace.

THE PULL FACTORS AT THE WORKPLACE

Learning does not stop at the end of a college degree; neither do you shelf your business ideas or tools and skills after completing your trade. There is lots more knowledge to garner, to be on the cutting edge of time. Modern times desire new ideas, strategies, computer savvy skills and technological intelligence, to compete with market forces. You have to be in competition with the world best and you are in it to win.

You may wonder what a pull factor is. Well it is simple: things that draw you to a place, or factors that give you that magnetic attraction to something. You may also describe it as things that influence you to want to stay, stick to the job you love or to an event at hand. These pull factors may be: performance-based pay; computer-technological equipped workplace; overtime pay and positive working environment; and good ergonomics, competency and motivation on the job.

Performance-based workplace atmosphere allows you to bring out the best in you, produce high quality products, and be well paid. It is task-oriented, demands high-grade work and attracts the highest-paying jobs. It also attracts experts in their field of work or studies, with competency and efficiency, someone who is a professional in their areas that makes little or no room for mistakes in their work. Most times, they have high expectations of their work and working conditions, providing the ideal tools, equipment and environment to work. Hence, high performance and excellent result is the hallmark.

Competency in your area is paramount to getting the job done, such as skills set and knowledge in a particular field. Whenever you are competent, it means you have a high level of mastery in your area and can deliver the best outcome at all times, given the right ergonomics.

Motivation is a vital component to accelerate the work rate in any business. This relates to things used to let you feel uplifted or your morale to be on a high at work. This may be when someone makes a compliment or praise for the job well done. It may be an incentive, extra pay or promotion in the job. This could be high paying company that offers good salary, benefits or payment by performance.

They are many times employees may procrastinate or delay the rate at which a task can be done. For example, a friend needs a letter of claims from his insurance company. This letter would be needed by his prospective insurance company in less than three days' time in order for the rebate on the total cost of insurance premium. Quite interestingly, the administrative secretary refused from honoring the request by the client. She blatantly said no! "Sir, come back for the letter in the next time five days."

This does not make sense; why should a client wait for another five days? Whereas after three days, that said letter would be useless or not valid to get such benefit. Imagine: all the other documents were in place to get the job done. You see, employees tend to delay their work rate, which does not bring dividends to a company or equity to the client. It was upsetting to the client who needs a simple letter of claims, yet most importantly, to accomplish his business.

The client had no option but to plead his case with the secretary and politely explain to her stating the far journey traveled: by far over 50 miles distance, back and forth. The client emphasizing further that the letter is needed within the next three days in order to get claim benefits. The client said: "I am asking you, PLEASE, see how you can help me?" After listening to the client plead, the young lady said quickly, "Sir, I am asking you to sit down and wait. Within the next five minutes you will get the letter." In exactly five minutes the client was given the letter of claims.

IMPORTANCE OF WORK RATE IN THE WORKPLACE

Certainly! You can clearly see shared attitudes on the path of the administrative secretary and the client. The client showed up with an attitude of purpose, attitude of persistency and humility. These positive attitudes were able to counteract and overcome the delayed tactics. The secretary displayed negative work attitudes towards her client in her approach, one of inefficiency, hostility and lackadaisical attitude. But the client was able to bring out the best in her: that of resilience and mental toughness to come through on her work rate.

Your work rate as an employee takes in many factors that stimulate the ability to function effectively in the workplace. These factors include: good nutrition, which will foster concentration and endurance; physical health /fitness; skill training; and speed efficiency. Any employer will be ready to employ an individual, who has good work attitude and skill sets to produce the best output within the shortest time given.

Let's say, you have a company with a high demand for a typist; requires two ladies for the job as a typist; and gives all criteria and requirements made known and available to them. One of the criteria is that: Typist must be able to type 100 words in five minutes. After going through the interview, you see that on the practical assessment, you recognized that both finish the task but one of the interviewees completed 100 words in four minutes, while the other person completed 100 words in six minutes.

It is most definite that the lady with the better work rate of 100 words in four minutes would be the lady of choice to get the job. If no one else turns up, it means that another interview would have to be reconvened to get someone to meet the minimum required work rate of the company. Let's settle for the best.

HOW WORK RATE ATTITUDE INFLUENCE PRODUCTIVITY.

An economist developed a mathematical formula of the 80/20 principle. This principle describes the unequal distribution of wealth in his country. This law is a vital instrument to use as a guide to prioritize and manage our work in life. This 20/80 as above rule means: in any situation, 20 percent of the inputs or activities are responsible for 80 percent of the outcomes. In this situation, it meant that 20 percent of the people owned 80 percent of the wealth. This is suggesting that 80 percent of the people are in the poor class of this society.

HOW CAN THIS 20/80 PERCENT PRINCIPLE APPLY TO OUR EVERYDAY LIFE?
This principle is a powerful tool that can be used and apply in almost every sphere of our life. It will eventually unfold some stunning discoveries about how to solve many of the problems in our life and society.

Let us look at areas where this principle can be useful, for example in our Social Studies at a school. If you are doing a course in Social Studies, in the exam you can look at the questions to see how the marks are allotted, and the questions that carry the most marks. Then you do them first because they will allow you to get to a passing grade quicker or finish in a faster time.

In general, most times in a subjective exam, the 20/80 rule is applied. Twenty percent of the higher marks are accounted for 80 percent of the exam grade or result. Likewise, in a particular subject area, sometimes when studying, 80 percent of what you study for you do not see reflected in relevant exam questions; only 20 percent yield the results. This means you have wasted most time on areas that you did not have to study. Managing your energy or effort is very important; if you can put more of your energy on areas that give better result, you will be more productive and on a successful path than wasting time on something that is non-productive.

The principle of the 80/20 is a practical rule if applied effectively; it can yield prosperous outcome in most circumstances. Let us look at, how you can acquire money by using this principle. Take for example, if you are working two streams of incomes. If income (A) is your main stream of income, it is earning you $2,500 per day. Income (B) earning is from a grocery shop, bringing in a total of $10,000 per day. Income (A) is derived from a five days' workweek while, Income (B) is derived from a two days per week effort.

It therefore means the grocery shop will produce more money per day, which indicates less time /effort is used to gain more money per month. This sum total would be approximately $80,000 per month. The better result of both streams of income is the business, which in fact reveals the job that takes more effort and time is the 9 to 5 and fewer earnings: $50 000 per month. The grocery shop takes less effort and yields better earnings.

Use the information you read from the chapters of this book to fill in the most suitable answers.

Questions:

1. Explain the 80/20 principle.

2a. List two areas of your life in which the 80/20 principle can be applied.

2b. Explain how you will apply these two 80/20 principle listed to your life?

CHAPTER 9

"Life is an interesting journey, likened to the four seasons of the year: spring, summer, autumn, winter. You can work in all the seasons if you can. But if you want to win and overcome life struggles, let's look at the wisdom of the Ant. She works in the summer and rests in the winter. It will not always be sunshine, so plan your future wisely as the ant."

—P.Reid

There is a beauty about the creation of man, called the human body: the unique way how the big five senses are designed and how each sense is positioned in the body. This tells a great story of planning, organization and the meticulous execution of the work of the potter. I just imagine how the master potter must have felt after the completion of the first framework: Adam. He must have felt pleased with his finished work; all the parts were in their rightful places and functioning at its best. It was looking good. We are not sure what season Adam was created or whether it was in spring, summer, autumn or in winter time. How long did it take the creator? We don't know. Have you ever, wondered what season was it? Think about it...

You may be asking yourself the question too: what is the big five?

HOW ATTITUDE INFLUENCES WORK AND PRODUCTIVITY

Frankly speaking the big five are your primary senses of perception: the sense of feeling, seeing, hearing, smelling and tasting.

Some brilliant scholars opine that there may be a sixth sense called "common sense." The pundits think common sense is also vital because it makes you smarter than those who did not develop this extra sense. But since this cannot be scientifically proven, we have to contend with what we know or what you may have clarity of information about, accepting the idea for what it worth.

The senses of the body are the essential sensory perceptions which perk up various codes from the brain, process them and let you know what is happening in the environment or world at large. They complement each other; all five senses can be working all at one time, so long each is in excellent health condition.

—◆—

Positive coordinated approaches among these senses are marvelous. For example, I might be looking at someone while I am also feeling the warmth of the sunlight on the skin, taking in some vitamin-D from the electrified ultra violet rays of the sun. Julian may be running all day and feeling hot and tired so, while she is resting, she is sipping a bottle of lucozade drinks. Julian is experiencing the use of the sense of feeling: the heat of the day and the sense of taste testifying to the sweetness or bitterness of the drink, as she sipped at the same time. What a masterpiece of art of work: a contrast of emotions!

WHAT ARE THE SENSES?

The senses are the physiological capacities of an organism to provide data for perception. The nervous system has a specific sensory system or organ dedicated to each sense. Sight, or vision, refers to the ophthalmoception, hearing audioception, taste gustaoception smell olfacoception, touch, and tactioception. How powerful are the works of these five beautiful senses? Each sense was designated with a specific attitude of purpose in the body.

The eyesight is one of the greatest senses in the human being. The ophthalmoception deals with the sensory perception of vision; it is one of the main sensory organs that possesses magnetic attraction and connection to all the other senses of the body. Whenever a person's sight is functioning properly, it makes one feels confident and powerful, like you can conquer the world. The sense of sight allows clarity to see and read information, observing a person's actions, an object or things, insects and lower class of animals, etc.

THE BIG FIVE SENSES NECESSARY FOR WORK

Sense of feeling is attached to the organ of perception called tactioception. This sense of feeling is operated through the sensory nervous systems. All five senses are attached to the nervous systems. The connection plays a pivotal role in each sense organ. The sense of feeling is expressed your emotions, which are subsequently aligned also with the word touch and use interchangeable with feeling. In any case, one sense of feeling is expressed in the emotions of a person, like feeling of hurt, anger, sadness, mourning, such as when you are in a bad mood it shows off through your negative attitude.

Furthermore, on the other hand the sense of feelings can be an expression of happiness, joy, excitement, pleasantry, kindness, enthusiasm, gladness and hope, and so on denote positive attitudes. An individual feeling is an expression coming from the core of his subconscious mind; how he thinks or opines, whether negative or positive. Your emotion is expressed through his modal action to tell someone how you are feeling: hopeful or enthusiastic.

It gives us the perception of vision, opthalmoception, to see objects from near or a distance, both small and large things. Oh! How I am amazed at the power of sight, the human being possesses. Most people, if you were to ask them which of the big five they used most among the rest of senses, I think, they would choose sight as number one. You see, most of what people learn is by seeing, looking on some objects. One scientist stated that approximately 85% of what we learn is by visualization. So therefore, the learning style: a visual learner would be more efficient than the audio-learner in the ability of a learner to learn concepts.

THE FIVE SENSES IMPACT PRODUCTIVITY

Many people would rather look for something rather than hear about it, if they have a choice to do so. For example, if I am buying a dress for my spouse, I rather look at the dress to make a choice, than hearing about the size, color or even the brand. In order to make up my mind to buy or not to buy, especially, if I know her size and shape, length and the type dress she likes. Already, I would have already known her fashionable qualities, which would influence my decision. I like to give surprises to the one I love. The choice of buying a gorgeous dress that's looking fabulous to wear on a special occasion would be a delight to me.

The clear vision of a worker is most important to be effective on the job. We need good sight to do our work and for movement into various spaces: the reading of information, studying, and observation of pleasurable sceneries. Seeing something natural makes you feel convinced of reality. The obscurity of a worker's vision gives a negative attitude, which will be a deterrent to production and productivity in any shape or form. The sensory organ sight expresses the power of seeing. For example, if I have a ripe Saint Julian mango as a gift, supposedly I cannot see. But I can taste and feel. It means that I could not determine whether the mango has a worm or not, due to my disability. If my sight were intact everything would be all right. There is a power that lies in the sense of visibility. Just to see what you are doing or an appearance of a piece of work you have accomplished makes you feel great!

Miss Brown has some dainty dresses for sale. One of the first requests of a customer who want to purchase this tangible product from her. She would say to her, "Come and look at what I have. Then make your choice." You could feel the quality material, but you would not be convinced to buy until you see the dress for yourself or you have someone to look at it and help you to make an informed decision.

—◦◆◦—

Audioception deals with the sense of hearing or the organ of perception. The ear includes the pinna or outer ear, inner ear, cochlea and eardrum make up that sensitive member. The ear is an organ of communication which collects information from the outside environment, processes them through the brain function and connect it with other sensory organs. The message/s recived by the ear are interpreted and conveyed through the mouth.

Most information received and learned by the ear is approximately 30% of what a normal human being would hear. This sensory organ is essential for the developing of one's faith. It is what you hear that gives you perceptions and a belief system to develop faith and trust in someone or thing. Whenever you understood something clearly, then this spiritual attitude of faith is exercised here. Faith is then placed into action and processes into reality.

CHAPTER 10

"People are the driving force of any company's success. If the employer takes care of worker's needs, they will take care of their business. If they are motivated to give their best at work., they will feel the vibes to give peak performance for the benefit to the company."

—P.Reid.

The He+M+S+A= P is the P.L. Reid's concept develop to show how high energy plus motivation plus speed/skills plus accuracy equals productivity. My observation of workers in different sectors of society over a twenty-year period has shown that this concept, which has been developed and highlighted are the basic components required for an efficient output of products within a company or any institution in the world at large.

He is a symbol in the formula, which means high energy food nutrients found in super food. These super nutrients are proteins, amino acids, phenylalanine, cysteine, histidine, isoleucine, methionine and lysine, carbs, minerals, vitamins and fats. Proteins are major nutrients which cause the growth and the maintenance of the tissues of the body. There are essential amino acids that are building blocks of proteins. Essential amino acids are obtained from proteins

HOW ATTITUDE INFLUENCES WORK AND PRODUCTIVITY

foods like legumes, peas/beans, meat, poultry and fish, etc.

Food is medicine and nutrition to our body. It helps to build and replenish the various systems of the human body. Nutritious food produces calories that give energy to the body, which is a constituent in every type of foods. The nutrients in food supply the body with a nutritive valve to build muscles, to fight off disease conditions and add high energy for physical functions of the body. For example, professional basketball players need high energy at every level to play their A game. Every fan of basketball knows the game is rigorous and the movement of the game is fast and it saps much of the player's energy. Therefore, basketball players need high energy to maintain their body to master of the game effectively. Proper dieting and meal preparation is highly recommended.

—◆—

A balanced meal must always contain protein and Amino acids, vitamins, minerals and carbohydrates. Basketball players need approximately 4-8 servings of fruits and vegetables per day to be at their optimum nutrient level and an intake of approximately 4-8 quarts of purified water per day to hydrate the system, for circulation and flushing the body of impurities. These nutrients give super energy and strength to each player, hence allowing them to perform at their best in a competition. There is power and stamina in these foods, which makes the individual player comes alive and keeps healthier.

THE IMPORTANCE OF
HE + M + S + A = P – CONCEPT TO WORKERS

Workers who are energized, skillful and highly motivated, will have a strong desire to work. Their attitude will be enhancing to work efficiently in their field of study. High energy will mobilize you into peak performance. It will keep you on top of your game. Your attitude of excelling will become consistent, always displaying a positive result. Good nutrition is important to workers. It stimulates the best performance at all times. Let's take in consideration an athlete who is running fast on the track. Most of his peers and even spectators will be upbeat about his performance. The question will be asked, "What are you eating?," similar to the Caribbean athlete ;Who eats yellow yams to get carbohydrate and Vitamin A to help develop muscles?

> Motivation –is like food to the mind and medicine to the body. It affects the psychic of the human being, lifting the morale to a higher plain. It takes a highly motivated employee to perform the objectives of the job effectively. The human being is made up of emotions: positive and negative. Sometimes, we are in high morale and at times on the other hand is cast down. When an individual is working with a low morale and not doing a good job, then encouragement or motivation will be necessary to boost him up into a better mood to do well. Employees need to know that food is a motivator. But he needs to know also where the motivation is needed most.

> If you are mentally drained, you need a mind booster, or physical fitness is a problem you need an exercise program or high energy to boost your health, good nutrition and stamina to be engaged in serious projects.

Skills –refer to your ability to do something well or if you are an expert in your craft. Skills are things you are gifted to do. For example: a trade, talent, a typist, graphic designer, auto-electrician, mechanic or writer etc. Some people are multi-skilled; they have the ability to do more than one thing or skill. This means you may be a mason by trade but you have the ability to do carpentry and be an electrician. In an age of technology, information and industry, where knowledge is rapidly increasing and traditional jobs are becoming obsolete. It is imperative that every young student must learn to be multi-task, even though they may be trained in a professional field complement it with a skill. To be relevant in today's society, the youths must be multi-skilled, learn fast, learn about new technologies and equip themselves to move with the time, to survive the economic conditions.

Speed –is the rate of progress, the motion of an object: how fast or slow it operates. It could also be how quick a person acts to do something. Workers' speed coupled together with accuracy shows the mastery of his skills. The population is on the increase; therefore, the need for products of different type are on the demand. So, workers have to meet supply of the consumers because, time is moving fast and it is said that time is money. When employees function efficiently, they will achieve a high productivity level.

Accuracy- is referring to the precision of menstrument, correct proportion in which you mixed a solution or make an object /product to suit the consumers. The customer is the main factor which must at all times be satisfied when producing and marketing a product. Your feasibility study must show what the consumers like in terms of size, quality taste etc., so you can manufacture to the needs and standards of the consuming public required. These four components are equivalent to productivity as the final results.

Desire – is a strong feeling of wanting to have something or wishing for something to happen. The desire of a person is in his mind or heart. A desire is a wish; it could be a pot of gold they want to be mined to realize material gain. Some desires need motivation but some may not. There are individuals who have desires, which can be either, one of the following:

- Store-up desires
- Workable desires

You will understand already that a store-up desire is a wish in static form, not activated. You may liken this scenario of desire to a fertile piece of land, not ploughed. It is just there, never worked or put to productive use.

In some cases, people call it virgin land: not touched. There are luminaries who have great ideas and visions and are never given a chance or take the opportunity to share them with others. Great abilities or possibilities not channeled into a positive outcome are dormant. Desires are locks in your subconscious mind that are creative ideas, just waiting to be stimulated by some positive motivation. This is a simply description of potential desires.

Written desires recorded on paper will not move, if you do not remove them to the next level. This level is the processing stage.

High-energy food has plenty of calories that are able to energize the worker. This energy level helps power the individual with super strength to withstand the task given to accomplish. Whenever individuals do not use up the required about of food nutrients to give the maximum energy, the workers will lapse in work turnover, causing lower output of work.

Workable desires are some things in motion you are actively engaged to put to work and fully utilize. These desires are like a clocks ticking away that never stop.

Mankind has several other types of desires that have being explored namely:

- Natural desires
- Spiritual desires
- Good desires
- Fulfilled desires

Natural desires are innate wishes or ideas you hope to bring into reality. You may have a dream house or condominium to build in the years to come. You put plans in place like your architectural drawings, foundational development and materials for construction. These intentions might not necessarily complete all at one time, but may be just work in progress.

Spiritual desires are faith-based supernatural ideology or beliefs which help to determine your moral standing. Faith is the substances of things hoped for and the evidence of things not seen. Your religious practices and culture guide your everyday life; your faith is paramount to achieve your desires. One may envision themselves becoming a Christian counselor or spiritual leader. These desires are very good spiritual inclinations but unless you work on these desires, they will not be realized by themselves. You need to nourish and train these desires, to bring them to fruition.

HOW DOES HE + M + S + A = P CONCEPT INFLUENCE PRODUCTIVITY?

Good desires are unsatisfied longings of an individual; they must be influenced by positive motivation so that these wishes may come into fruition. They can be dreams or visions of physical things intended to be developing into creative reality. When you have an idea in your mind and hope to achieve it within a reasonable period, that's your desire. For example, you wish to take a visit to Mount Everest. It's a great adventure that may never leave your mind, and you may be so excited to know something about it. How can I reach, and what will take you there? Researching, this attractive site would be a venture by itself, which should be a fascinating experience. In any case, it would worth the while doing.

Scientific researchers frequently have projects that they do research from time to time; Mount Everest is one of them. It does not just come with a desire only but a power of influence. It comes with the influence of purpose in regards to the natural resource found on the mountain and its benefits to the people of the country or visitors who tours the site. Just to think about climbing Mount Everest is a great challenge comparable to the skills, expertise and financial resources needed to do the research and get there.

Fulfilled desires are wishes achieved or carried out: things you once long to see, now come to pass or into fruition. For example, let's say your son at the age of fourteen told his mom he wanted to become a doctor when he grew up. Mom said, "This sounds good! Son keeps on dreaming." Little did mom know that his son had a plan. He went through high school and passed his eight required subjects with distinctions. He did not stop; he pursued his Cape courses to qualify his matriculate into university and also was successful. Henry's only hurdle was get financing for his medical training at med school. Mom was financially drained. He was a brilliant student with a good GPA, so he managed to get a scholarship and off to university. He was a smart worker, though he had challenges but he was able to overcome them. He went through med school, toiled hard and long but no sooner, he came out a proud son with his medical doctorate degree.

DISCOVER YOUR MEMORY POTENTIALS
Use the information you read from the chapters of this book to fill in the most suitable answer/s.

Questions:
Write down the definition of the word motivation.
How does motivation influence productivity?

THE WINNING ATTITUDES

CHAPTER 11

Winning attitude is a state of mind, wanting to put into action how to be victorious over something or someone. You feel like a winner when you practice the gems of winning. To win, it takes strength, courage and the push to be successful. The continuous practice of something will lead you into the attitude of winning all the time. Do you want to be winning?

Most companies are operating with approximately twenty percent of the amount of their people with winning attitudes. That they need to function efficiently on any given day. Using Pareto's 80/20 principle, it means that only 20 percent of the workforce is with the winning attitude, carrying out the bulk of the production, while the rest of 80 percent are under-performing. They do not have the positive work attitude and winning attitude to make the company operate on eight cylinders or at its maximum capacity. This means therefore, 80 percent of the workers need to adjust themselves to winning ways by adopting right attitudes that will enhance better productivity. Personal development is a must through training and mentoring from other co-workers with such required skills.

HOW ATTITUDE INFLUENCES WORK AND PRODUCTIVITY

Let's look at some.

Four Winning Attitudes that can transform the workplaces.:

- Attitude of purpose
- Positive attitude
- Mental attitude
- Attitude of gratitude

ATTITUDE OF PURPOSE

People exhibit actions daily at work, which helps to determine whether their attitude is purposeful or not. Attitude of purpose speaks to a cause for doing something, plan of action, goal setting, and a sense of direction. An individual with attitude of purpose is business-like and uses good communication skills. He is organized and proactive in his approach to life, and knows what they are about. Workers who have an attitude of purpose are exemplified above the rest, show good work ethics, high level of professionalism and produce higher quality work and efficiency. The employee who is purposeful manages his time well, is punctual at work and meetings, and knows his job: someone who does have regards for his work, and is right on target with his business.

POSITIVE ATTITUDE

Positive attitude is the lifeblood of winning at the workplace or reaching your goal. Every employee must possess the mind to win. They must work with the same aim, teamwork spirit, and a good communication link or interpersonal relationship skills. It should be the hallmark of every person to wear a positive image, produce quality work and make proper use of time. Faith is a gem everyone should have, a level of faith and the same vision of the company's goal. Everyone has a level of faith depending on your belief system. And you should believe in yourself and your company. You should have the knowledge of the goodness in the universe and what it has to offer. A person who has faith and vision of what he wants to do and where he wants to go will eventually know the steps and how to timely get there. Employees with a positive team spirit and willingness to work will make the dream works.

Grace is also a winning attitude; it is an exceptional feeling of love or favour causing people to feel belong and connected to you. It expresses a beautiful feeling of compassion to our fellowmen, to give and care for another person and a good mind towards their welfare. When grace is expressed and shared among us; it affects our sense of human relations and camaraderie, which illuminates your life forever. People who exhibit such attitudes of grace are always positive and hopeful. They are proactive, wanting to get the job done. They never seem to have a bad day, always full of smiles now and then but when the day is over, their task is always completed. The attitude of grace sends positive energy and a compelling influence to keep you going on a successful path.

MENTAL ATTITUDE

Mental attitude is your intelligence, brainpower and strength of character: how effectively one can utilize knowledge in a skillful way. There are moods of mental attitude that produce winning results in any situation, namely peace, love, faith and hope. These attitudes create a sense of consciousness in decision making. Whenever employees have a peaceful disposition, it fosters good communications, human relationships among your peers and a better productive atmosphere. This modal attitude spans across boundaries among staffs, supervisors, and managers causing greater working relationship and understanding.

The emotions or feeling of an individual has a link with one's mental attitude, which means much to how one behaves. Everyone needs to be loved and loves to be care for and also likes to feel important. My friend, it is not what you say or even what you do to a person matters but how you make the person feel that counts. The workplace at times can be very morbid or cold. But if employer can just let each employee feel loved and important, valuing their expertise, work and time, I just imagine, you would have almost done half of the task ahead. There must be a created atmosphere with that synergy at the workplace which propels each person to work without being pushed by a task master.

Mental attitude is the intellectual capacity to respond positively to circumstances that may arise. Many employees try to build their capacity by reading a storybooks, playing chess, and learning five new words from the dictionary to keep their mental sharpness. Some may do short courses or build their skills areas. You see, employees want to be at their best on the job, so creating a happy, peaceful, confident and passionate experience is key. These are feelings experienced by everyone in our day-to-day life journey in society: better yet at work. These feelings sometimes affect productivity, either in a positive or negative way. There are times as a person you feel like sharing moments of relaxation in a calm, quiet place with friends and family. You can exchange thoughts of past times, which will foster pleasant memories and experiences, never to be forgotten. A peaceful mind is an effective ammunition to silence the rage of violence. It can still the raging waves and shattered the attempts of war. When someone is quiet and relaxed, he will have that mental poise or attitude, to choose the right words to manipulate the flare of verbal conflict. It could be to smooth the rough edges of someone violent and boisterous behavior at work. But mental toughness helps workers to make good decisions in his life.

Use the information you read from the chapters of this book to fill in the most suitable answer/s.

Questions:

What are winning attitudes?

List 4 winning attitudes.

Why are winning attitudes necessary in the workplace?

CHAPTER 12

"Extra-ordinary people do great things that look special. They stand up and stand out of the crowd. But ordinary persons do simple things and always look for someone to lean on."

—P. Reid

Smart workers are quick thinkers, witty or clever people. They portray a spirit of boldness and confidence. They are sharp and love to solve problems in their field. They know what they are doing.

Smart workers can easily be identified. They are wise and tactful. They are also classified as gifted and skillful in what they do best.

Good workers know their art well and use the right tool to solve the problem. Smart workers think of solutions more frequently than the problem to be solved. Hence, the problem consumes less of their energy, therefore giving you more time and energy to work on the solution. This makes your effort worthwhile. When one can find many solutions for one problem, that great! You are even smarter at your art; when you can use different methodologies to arrive at same solution, you are hyper-skilled.

HOW ATTITUDE INFLUENCES WORK AND PRODUCTIVITY

Just be creative, articulating your smart ideas into real live materialistic functions. It makes you feel awesome! When you can touch people's lives by helping them to find solutions to their many challenges, it feels fulfilling. It brings satisfaction and a stupendous sense of accomplishment in life.

To be smart, you must possess the following qualities: be a critical thinker, highly skillful, efficient worker, knowledgeable, quick understanding and gifted.

Whenever the case arises, smart worker take on challenges any time convenient, especially, in their skill set and field of study. Smart workers respond where there is an opportunity and at times at work they tend to act in sporadic moment.

THE QUALITIES OF SMART WORKERS

Smart workers are brilliant persons with excellent intelligence quotients. They function at high levels; most smart workers like to work on their own. They are gifted, love to solve technical problems; they are innovator /scope thinkers and always have creative ideas to share with serious and interesting people. Most times, they learn from experience in the environment and use their common sense.

HOW TO IDENTIFY SMART WORKER?

Working smart means you act in a clever or intelligent way when working. Smart workers' way of doing things is above the normal or they are scope thinkers. Smart people do smart things: they are just brilliant, cunning and skillful. Their intelligence quotient (I.Q.) seems much sharper and quicker in solving any problems; what might be difficult to some people, they find it simple or for a better word, easy. They seem to get some cute names that are short and funny to pronounce. For example, the light bulb was developed by a brilliant innovator and inventor; he was smart.

Smart workers are quick thinkers and keen observers when working on objects or problems. In many circumstances, they are relaxed, analytical and capable of mastering their art and finding solutions for your problems in short order. It is beneficial when you can utilize your skills wisely, managing your time efficiently and using small resources with little effort to maximize production in your business. Certainly! You are smart. Smart people like to do difficult things or challenges, making them into a simple exercise. Some people think smart workers are weird at times.

HOW SHOULD YOU TREAT A SMART WORKER?

Smart persons are normal human being and must be treated as such; they may be gifted with special abilities but they are still normal individuals. They are not easily carried away by compliments or praise, because they see the problem they solved as normal, while you may see it as special and a big deal. They are an asset to any company and country in which they work. They are the catalyst and motivating force to production in any factory or company. Smart employees are seeing and treated as experts. They are generally remunerated to match their quality performance on the job. They get the lucrative contracts available at most times.

IT IS IMPORTANT
TO KEEP SMART WORKERS IN WORKPLACE

- Smart worker are an asset to a company.
- They are skillful and efficient in their field.
- They are sharper than the ordinary worker; they have command over their skills set.
- They are influential and attract quality customers to any company.
- Smart workers are efficient at what they do best.

Smart employers always look for the expert, professional, skilled and smart workers needed in factories and industrial companies across the world. These calibre of workers are the core: people who are great assets to companies in developing and first world countries. Their skillful expertise commands the attention and respect of CEOs and management in companies that demand quality employees of such illustrious career. When a company has such influential quality experts, they are held as an asset. The smart innovators help to accelerate the productivity within the workplace. The smart people are always sought after and held in high esteem because they help to drive performance at the workplace.

HOW DO SMART WORKERS
INFLUENCE PRODUCTIVITY?

- Smart workers are go-getters and the propelling force behind production.
- They are the trendsetters who will get the job done.
- Smart workers are leaders and they are targeted as motivators to others.

- They do outstanding work and their work speak well of them.
- Smart workers are positive thinkers and they command the respect of their employer /employees.

There are many smart workers in our world today. Sometimes, we called them other names like gifted, quick-scope thinkers and innovators. They are gifted in the sense that they possess abilities and skills, which supersede persons of similar ability. Smart workers are exceptional in skill sets; they are the catalyst and influential force to productivity. They are trendsetters and motivators who enhance the productivity in any factory or industry of a country. Smart workers are leaders in their field of study that they practiced. As a matter of fact, they are the inventors who develop new products, trained and supervisor workers to make an impact and carry out efficient work and productivity in some of these big companies.

Smart workers are not necessarily formally trained in everything they studied or practiced. But they are incidental learners who learn along the way. They do investigative learning, where they follow patterns and cause and effect methods to find a solution to a particular challenge. Smart workers think differently; they think out of the box to arrive at workable solutions to a problem. They are always researching to find new and different methods to solve cases that arise from time to time.

Use the information you read from the chapters of this book to fill in the most suitable answer/s. Then, see if there are ideas you have gleaned, which could help you to make a greater success in your life.

Questions:
1. Who would you define as a smart worker?
2. How can you identify a smart worker?
3. Why is it important to keep smart employees in the work-place?

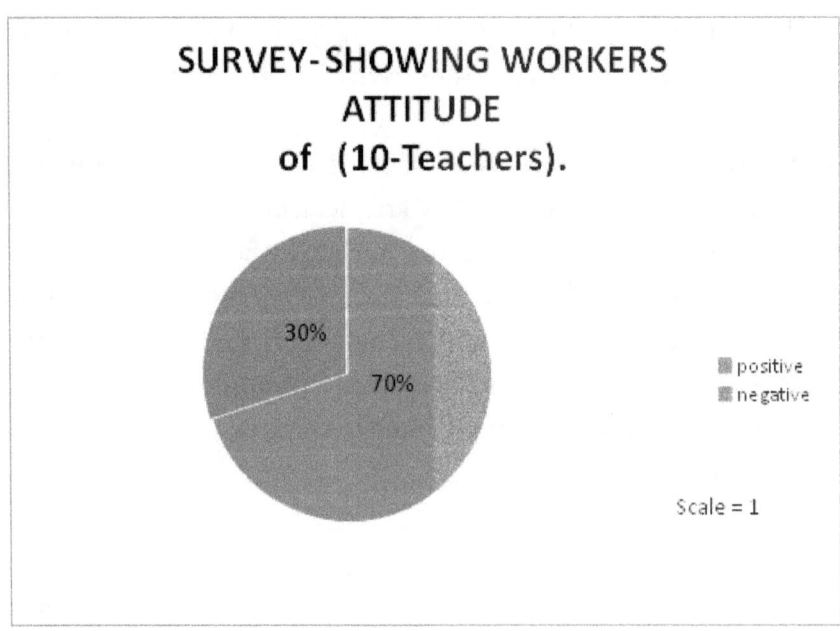

CHAPTER 13

The circle in diagram represents ten (10) teachers as samples, expressed as fractions and as percentage (out of 100). Three teachers expressed a negatively queued responses and seven teachers expressed a positively queued responses to questions given in the survey; which means that, there is a ratio of 3: 7, orange to blue respectively, or $3/7 = 3x10 = 30$, $/7x10 = 70 = 30/70$. When the ratio is calculated, the scale factor is,10. This could be equated to 1 teacher sample to 10 representations /hundred expressed above.

This survey was done on workers attitude –both positive and negative.

It was conducted on ten classroom teachers. These brilliant classroom teachers were so, willing to participate in this survey on attitude. The teachers were from two groups of Public school,

Primary and Secondary schools. The majority of the teachers were working at Primary school.

This sample of 10 –ten workers were meant to represent 100 or one hundred teachers. Ratio: 1:10. Because attitude of workers is vital

HOW ATTITUDE INFLUENCES WORK AND PRODUCTIVITY

in their everyday activity. It becomes an interested topic to survey and make findings to qualify some behavioral responses of individual employees.

Most Importantly to use some of these finding as target pointers, that can be corrected by applicable solution. Each participant in this survey was given ten (10) statements to respond to say whether they-(agree or disagree). These statements consist of both positive and negative attitudes in the areas which this book is written. The primary areas of concentration are work attitude, time management, attitude of purpose, attitude of acceptance, mental attitude, smart workers and winning attitude.

DISCOVER YOUR MEMORY POTENTIAL

Use the information you read from the chapters of this book to fill in the most suitable answer/s.

Questions:
1. What are the negative attitudes you portrayed that turn off your boss?
2. List four positive attitudes you have that caused others to follow you.
3. List four new things you read about that will help to motivate you in the workplace.
4. Name two main things that resonate from this book that affect your life.

5 PHOBIAS PEOPLE POSSESS

Phobias are fears that cause people to display some irrational behaviors or attitude. Namely:

- Trypophobia – fear of holes.
- Aerophobia – fear of flying.
- Mysophobia – fear of germs.
- Claustrophobia – fear of enclosed space.
- Acrophobia – fear of snakes.

REFERENCES OF READINGS

Bible – King James Version.

Hill Napoleon, – Think & Grow Rich. 1883-1970.

Maxwell John, C. 5 Levels of Leadership

Meyers Paul J. – 24 keys That Bring Complete Success.

www.ingramcontent.com/pod-product-compliance
Lightning Source LLC
Chambersburg PA
CBHW061513180526
45171CB00001B/161